WHO'S REALLY ON THESE DATING APPS

Uncovering Love, Lies, and Digital Deception

Written By

Amelia L. Starwell and Nicholas J. Matyas

"Behind every profile is a person, but not always the whole truth. The hesitation many feel is not weakness; it is awareness shaped by experience. In digital spaces where appearance can be curated and intentions concealed, discernment becomes necessary. Yet even after disappointment or deception, the longing to be met with honesty and kindness remains, enduring and unwilling to disappear"

- Santiago Dagon

The Discovery Walkabout Collection Of Reflective Writing

WHO'S REALLY ON THESE DATING APPS?

Library of Congress Control Number:

Paperback ISBN: 978-1-971561-05-9

E-Book ISBN: 978-1-971561-06-6

First Edition 2026

Cover design and layout by Discovery Walkabout Studio

Published by Discovery Walkabout Press

Printed in the United States of America

For permission requests, inquiries, information about educational licensing, collaborations, events, speaking, or reprint rights, contact:

Discovery Walkabout Press https://discoverywalkabout.com

Legal Information and Disclaimer

This book contains references to studies, organizations, companies, platforms, publications, and quotations believed to be accurate at the time of writing. The authors have made a good faith effort to present information that is factual, fair, and balanced.

Some material in this book reflects analysis, interpretation, opinion, or observation. These viewpoints may be based on the author's personal experiences, on experiences shared by others, or on publicly available research and reporting. Such perspectives are offered for informational and educational purposes and should not be construed as statements of fact about any individual or entity.

The inclusion or mention of any organization, company, platform, or study does not imply endorsement, criticism, or wrongdoing unless explicitly stated. All trademarks and names are the property of their respective owners.

Despite careful research and review, errors or omissions may occur. If a factual discrepancy is identified, the authors and publisher are committed to addressing it promptly and fairly. Where appropriate, corrections or clarifications will be issued in future editions or public updates.

Nothing in this book is intended as legal, financial, or professional advice. Readers are encouraged to verify information independently and to exercise their own judgment when interpreting the material presented.

Terminological Clarification: "Online Dating" and the Nature of Introduction

For clarity, this book uses the term **online dating** in its conventional sense while making an important distinction between introduction and dating itself.

Digital dating platforms do not facilitate dating in the literal or experiential sense. Rather, they function as systems of introduction, connecting individuals who would otherwise be unlikely to encounter one another within their existing social, geographic, or professional networks. These platforms enable initial contact, profile-based screening, and mediated communication, but they do not constitute dating as it is commonly understood in social or relational contexts.

Dating occurs when two individuals meet in person and engage in shared experience. It involves embodied interaction, emotional exchange, behavioral observation, and mutual decision-making, elements that cannot be fully replicated or evaluated through digital interfaces. Online interaction may precede dating, but it does not replace it.

The continued use of the term **online dating** reflects historical and cultural evolution rather than technical accuracy. Early personal advertisements, matchmaking services, and later algorithmic platforms were framed around romantic and sexual intent, not casual social connection. As a result, the language of dating persisted even as the function of these systems remained primarily introductory.

Throughout this book, online platforms are therefore treated as introductory mechanisms rather than as sites of dating itself. This distinction is essential for understanding user expectations, emotional responses, and the structural limitations of these technologies. Confusion between introduction and dating often contributes to misplaced expectations, emotional fatigue, and misunderstandings about progress, commitment, and intimacy in digitally mediated relationships.

Historical Background of This Book

The original manuscript for this book was written in 2001, rewritten again ten years later in 2011. Both remained unpublished. And, in 2026 it was rewritten again. It has now been extensively updated to reflect the dramatic changes in dating and digital culture over the past twenty-five years. Yet the central question remains unchanged:

WHO'S REALLY ON THESE DATING APPS?

Dating in the late 1940s, there was no email, no texting, no social media. If a man wanted to ask a woman on a date, he wrote a letter, made a phone call on a rotary dial telephone, or knocked on her door. Social expectations were structured and clear. In many homes, asking a woman's parents first was still considered respectful.

By the late 1970s, the social world was shifting. Women were gaining empowerment. College culture was evolving. Yet communication tools were still simple. There were no cell phones or email. If you were interested in someone, you called or met in person.

The early 2000s changed everything. Cell phones, texting, email, and social networking became routine. Handwritten letters disappeared. Courtship moved onto screens.

In 2001, we wrote "Internet Dating has opened the fable Pandora box of possibilities that erases all pre-existing and limiting geographical, cultural, religious, and ethical barriers."

In 2011, we wrote "Internet Dating has thrown a new curveball into the interpersonal landscape. Internet dating sites allow users to communicate anonymously with one another in a cloak and dagger fashion hidden behind profiles which or may not reveal someone's true intent."

By 2026, what once felt futuristic now feels routine. Online dating gathers countless possibilities into a single swipe, guided by algorithms and artificial intelligence that increasingly shape who we see.

But technology has only changed the meeting place, not human nature. The chance of meeting someone unethical online is no greater than meeting them at work, on the street, or even in a church. Character still unfolds the same way it always has. Slowly.

Time, attention, and caution remain our best guides. In any garden, patience reveals which blooms are real and which hide thorns.

Each generation followed its own dating sequence:

G.I. Generation

Mail → Face to face

Silent Generation

Mail → Face to face → Phone

Baby Boomers

Face to face → Mail → Phone

Generation X

Phone → Email → Face to face

Millennials

Texting → Social media → Online platforms → Face to face

Generation Z

Social media → Texting → Online platforms → Face to face

As communication accelerated, clarity declined. There is no longer a single "correct" way to approach someone. Every person carries personal communication preferences. Often, how someone prefers to receive communication differs from how they give it.

When the original manuscript was written in 2001, digital dating felt new. Caution was lighter. Today, experience has reshaped that innocence. Technology has widened access to connection, but it has also widened opportunity for manipulation.

The early principles offered in 2001 remain relevant because human nature has not changed.

2001 Internet Dating Observations

Face to Face Still Matters3

Words are easy. Action requires intention. Someone unwilling to meet, within reasonable and safe limits, may be avoiding transparency.

Communication Is Reciprocal

Healthy connection involves exchange. If someone consistently gathers information but reveals little, caution is warranted.

Emotional Clarity Matters

Love carries risk. Anyone unwilling to discuss feelings, expectations, or boundaries may not be prepared for genuine connection.

Growth Requires Accountability

Past hurt does not guarantee future harm. But a refusal to self-reflect often signals deeper issues.

Move With Awareness

Digital introductions typically move from messages to phone calls to in person meetings. Watch for alignment between words and actions.

Technology evolves. Human behavior adapts. But the underlying question remains:

In a world of profiles and algorithms, who is really behind the screen?

INTRODUCTION

Who We Become When We Search for Love Online

There is a quiet but powerful moment many people experience when creating a dating profile for the first time. The screen glows with possibility. The promise of connection feels close, almost tangible. Hope rises easily. So does vulnerability.

Online dating emerged in the mid-1990s, with platforms such as Match.com introducing the idea that strangers could meet through a computer screen. What began as compatibility questionnaires and cautious email exchanges slowly evolved into rapid swiping and algorithm driven matches. When mobile apps transformed the landscape in the early 2010s, meeting someone online shifted from unusual to normal. Today it is often the default.

Human beings have always searched for partnership. Ancient matchmaking traditions, arranged marriages, personal ads, and community introductions all reflect the same longing. What has changed is the speed, scale, and structure of the search.

Modern dating apps encourage quick decisions. A photograph. A short bio. A few curated details. Swipe left. Swipe right. The design suggests simplicity. Match. Message. Meet. Yet many users describe a different reality. Ghosting. Misrepresentation. Emotional confusion. Burnout. Some speak of loneliness that deepens even while conversations multiply.

Behind every profile stands a person. But not always the full truth.

This book asks a direct question: Who is really on these dating apps?

Together, we examine the digital ecosystem that shapes modern courtship. We explore how platform design influences behavior. We analyze the rise of deception, emotional misalignment, and manipulation. We look at the psychological forces that draw sincere seekers, casual browsers, married individuals, scammers, and the chronically unavailable into the same virtual space.

Our aim is not cynicism. It is clarity.

Online dating can lead to meaningful relationships. Many couples have met this way. But clarity matters. Awareness matters. Understanding the structure behind the screen matters.

This work draws from decades of lived dating experience, combined with global conversations, private testimonies, and extensive research into digital behavior and platform design. As authors, we bring both male and female perspectives to the discussion. What emerges is not accusation, but examination. Not fear, but informed caution.

Some chapters read as investigative analysis. Others feel more personal and reflective. The blend is intentional. Data reveals patterns. Experience reveals consequences.

If you choose to participate in online dating, we want you to do so with open eyes. Not hardened. Not naive. Informed.

The question is no longer whether digital dating is here to stay. It is.

The question is who you are meeting, how the system shapes the interaction, and how to protect both your heart and your judgment in the process.

CONTENTS

Part I The Digital Love Industry: How It Really Works 1

Chapter 1 The Business Of Loneliness 3

Chapter 2 Who Owns The Apps That Shape Your Love Life 9

Chapter 3 How Dating Apps Make Money Off Your Heart 17

Part II The Many Faces On Dating Apps: Who You Are Really Swiping On 25

Chapter 4 The Seven Major User Types 27

Chapter 5 The Hidden Groups Within Platforms 35

Chapter 6 The Rebounders, The Broken, And The Disguised 43

Part III The Dark Side: Deception, Scams, And Manipulation 49

Chapter 7 The Truth About Online Cheating 51

Chapter 8 The Scam Industry Behind Dating Apps 59

Chapter 9 Spotting The Crooked, The Dangerous, And The Toxic 65

Part IV The Apps Themselves: What They Promise Vs. What They Deliver 75

Chapter 10 Tinder: The Illusion Of Endless Options 77

Chapter 11 Bumble, Hinge, Match, And The "Relationship Apps" 85

Chapter 12 Okcupid, Pof, Facebook Dating, And Free Platforms 95

Chapter 13 Asian Dating Apps And International Platforms 103

Part V Truth, Safety, And Real Connection...................... 113

Chapter 14 Is Online Dating Really For You?................... 115

Chapter 15 How To Protect Yourself Online 121

Chapter 16 Alternatives To Online Dating For Finding True Love... 131

Chapter 17 What Real Love Requires That Dating Apps Cannot Give... 139

Chapter 18 Dating Tips For Each Generation Group 149

Conclusion A Clearer Path To Real Love 153

Acknowledgements 155

About Authors 157

Discovery Walkabout Press 159

PART I

THE DIGITAL LOVE INDUSTRY:

HOW IT REALLY WORKS

CHAPTER 1

THE BUSINESS OF LONELINESS

There is an uneasy stillness that sits inside many people before they ever download a dating app. It is not always fear of the unknown. Sometimes it feels more like a slight ache that grows in the late evenings when the home is still and the mobile phone screen glows nearby. That lonely heart ache may whisper a simple thought. Perhaps there is someone out there for me. And perhaps technology can help me find them.

According to early digital history sources, the first major online dating site, Match.com, appeared in 1995. It joined a world where personal classified ads had already existed for decades in newspapers, simple paragraphs written by people searching for companionship. The move from print to screen seemed like an evolution rather than a revolution. Yet it changed everything. Suddenly strangers who lived thousands of miles apart could send messages to each other with a single click. These early sites used questionnaires and personal profiles. They did not rely on swiping or rapid judgment. They were built around slow reading, careful selection, and the hope that shared interests could spark connection.

As the internet grew, so did the belief that algorithms might know the heart better than the heart knows itself. According to technological research from that era, companies experimented with systems that attempted to match people based on compatibility formulas. It created the idea that love could be measured, sorted, and delivered through a digital screen. Santiago Dagon once wrote, "The heart seeks mystery, but the mind seeks pattern." Early online dating leaned heavily toward the mind. It tried to turn romance into a pattern that could be solved.

THE ORIGINS OF ONLINE DATING

When we look back, it seems almost like innocence. The slow pace. The long emails. The careful introductions. There was no swiping. No instant judgment. People often took time to read a profile fully before reaching out.

According to several industry reports from the late 1990s and early 2000s, millions of adults joined platforms such as Match.com and eHarmony as the decade progressed. These spaces built the foundation for everything that came later.

It did not take long before the seeds of modern technology overwhelmed the inexperienced lonely hearts. Profiles could be curated making it easier for users to find and understand. Personal details could be shaped with desirable traits. Expectations could rise quickly as people imagined ideal partners from small bits of information. Loneliness mixed with hope. And hope mixed with fantasy.

WHEN DATING BECAME BIG TECH

The landscape changed dramatically when smartphones became common. Dating moved from a desktop activity to something people could do while standing in line for coffee. According to technology analysts, the launch of Tinder in 2012 introduced a new model built around speed. Swiping became the new language of attraction. Decisions that once took minutes now took seconds. Sometimes less.

This speed transformed dating into something that might resemble a game. It introduced a sense of possibility that felt exciting, even addictive. People could access a near endless stream of faces, which might have created the illusion of abundance. But abundance can also become noise. It overwhelmed the senses and made it difficult to choose. Some users reported that they often felt more anxious after long swiping sessions than they felt before. The apps did not intend to create anxiety. Yet the structure itself, the continuous flow of options, may have contributed to a cycle of searching rather than connecting.

As dating entered the world of Big Data, companies adapted the same patterns seen in social media. These included notifications, reward loops, and engagement strategies. According to public financial filings, many dating platforms earn significant revenue from subscriptions, premium boosts, and paid features that increase visibility. This is not criticism. It is simply the design of the industry. It might help to understand that once dating became part of the technology economy, it began following the same incentives as any digital platform that thrives on repeat users.

LOVE AS A SUBSCRIPTION MODEL

This is where the business side becomes more visible. Dating apps often rely on steady engagement. When someone finds a lasting relationship, they may leave the platform. When someone feels discouraged, lonely, or hopeful again, they may return. According to several market reports, subscription upgrades and paid boosts have become major sources of revenue for many dating companies. The pattern may appear simple. The longer people search, the more likely they are to pay for enhanced features.

This does not mean the platforms are designed to prevent love. It simply means they function within a structure where user activity supports business growth. A cycle emerges. People search. They match. They lose momentum. They come back. They feel a spark. Then disappointment. Then hope again. It is a rhythm that may feel familiar to anyone who has spent time swiping late at night while trying not to lose faith. It must be remembered dating platforms are for-profit companies, not humanitarians with your best interest at heart.

Perhaps this raises a question that many readers have already felt. If love becomes part of a subscription model, how does that shape the way we look for it? Santiago Dagon once wrote, "If you search for love with the urgency of hunger, you may choose the nearest bread instead of the nourishment you truly need." This reflection seems fitting here. A subscription may speed up the search, but it cannot deepen the capacity for real connection.

THE EMOTIONAL ECONOMY

Dating platforms do something subtle. They respond to emotion. According to behavioral studies, users often return to dating apps during moments of loneliness, heartbreak, boredom, or curiosity. These are normal human experiences. They may appear in waves throughout life. What is interesting is that the platforms benefit from these emotional cycles because each return generates activity. More swipes. More messages. More engagement. And perhaps more purchases.

Again, this is not about criticism. It is simply the nature of digital economies. Social media grows through attention. Streaming platforms grow through hours watched. Dating apps grow through the constant search for connection. When break-ups occur, people often reenter the apps. When boredom rises, people check profiles. When uncertainty enters a relationship, some may look at what else is out there. Each of these moments fuels the emotional economy.

Closing Thought

Imagine sitting with a friend over coffee. They tell you that they spent two hours swiping last night because they felt lonely. They shrug. They may laugh. They may apologize for it. And you might say, "I understand. I have done that too." These are the moments when the emotional economy becomes real. The apps are not causing loneliness. They are simply present whenever loneliness visits.

As you move through this book, allow yourself to notice the patterns without judgment. You might feel that you have lived part of this story already. That is the beginning of awareness. And awareness is what helps you navigate this digital world with more calm, more clarity, and more truth.

CHAPTER 2

WHO OWNS THE APPS THAT SHAPE YOUR LOVE LIFE

Most people scroll through their phones and open a dating app without thinking much about where it came from. The interface feels familiar. The colors, the layout, the small icons that encourage swiping or messaging. These things seem simple, almost invisible. Yet behind that touch of a finger sits an entire corporate structure that shapes how love is offered, marketed, and filtered to millions of people.

According to public financial filings and industry reports, ownership in the dating world is far more consolidated than many users realize. A few companies hold a significant share of the digital relationship landscape. Many companies are publicly traded, meaning their shares are available for purchase on stock exchanges allowing anyone to invest in their growth. Match.com's parent company is Match Group, Inc., traded on NASDAQ under the ticker symbol MTCH. The Match Group owns a massive portfolio of popular dating apps and sites, including Tinder, Hinge, Match.com, OkCupid, Plenty of Fish, OurTime, and HER, offering diverse platforms for different demographics and relationship goals.

It may feel strange to think about love in terms of corporate ownership. And perhaps a little uncomfortable. But understanding who designs the apps may help you understand the environment you are stepping into. Santiago Dagon once wrote, "The path you walk matters as much as what you hope to find at the end." This chapter is meant to illuminate that journey.

THE MATCH GROUP EMPIRE

According to Match Group public filings, the company owns several of the most recognized dating platforms: Tinder, Hinge, Match.com, OkCupid, Plenty of Fish, OurTime, Meetic, BLK, Chispa, The League, Upward, and HER. eHarmony is owned by the ParshipMeet Group, a leading international online dating company. ParshipMeet Group owns major dating brands including matchmaking sites like eHarmony, Parship, and ElitePartner, alongside social/video dating apps from The Meet Group like MeetMe, Tagged, LOVOO, Skout, and GROWLr, offering a diverse portfolio for different connection types. SilverSingles is owned by Spark Networks, a major online dating company that operates several brands for different demographics, including EliteSingles, Zoosk, Jdate, and ChristianMingle. When people move from one app to another, they often remain within the same corporate ecosystem, even if it feels like they are entering a new world.

This does not mean the apps are identical. Each platform grew up with its own personality. Tinder introduced the swipe culture that reshaped online dating. Match.com built a foundation around profiles and search. OkCupid leaned toward questionnaires and values-based matching. Hinge promoted meaningful conversation with its prompt-driven format. Plenty of Fish offered a wide-open social arena with fewer constraints. These differences may feel significant to users, yet the same Match Group parent company oversees how each platform evolves.

Imagine sitting at a café with a friend who says, "I deleted Tinder. I am trying Hinge now. It seems different." You may smile and say, "Different house, same neighborhood." The friend might laugh. It is human nature to seek a fresh start, even when the architecture behind the scenes has not changed.

The reason so many apps sit under one corporation is simple. According to several business analyses, consolidation allows for shared technology, unified data insights, cost efficiency, and stronger market control. For users, this might mean smoother interfaces and faster innovation. It also means that a smaller number of companies influence the romantic experiences of millions. It also means they have access to personal information about users. Match.com states they don't sell user data and follow ISO 27001 security standards, an international standard providing a framework for establishing, implementing, maintaining, and continually improving an Information Security Management System (ISMS) to protect data confidentiality, integrity, and availability.

THE INDEPENDENT PLATFORMS

Not every major dating app belongs to a large parent company. According to company histories and industry data, several platforms remain independent or semi-independent. Bumble positioned itself as a women-first platform, giving women the power to message first. Bumble Inc., the parent company of the Bumble, Badoo, and Fruitz dating apps, is publicly traded on the NASDAQ stock exchange under the ticker symbol BMBL. Bumble Inc.'s corporate headquarters are located in Austin, Texas.

SilverSingles and Elite Singles built themselves around mature daters and professional matchmaking. SilverSingles and EliteSingles are both owned by Spark Networks SE, a global online dating company that also owns other popular apps like Zoosk, ChristianMingle, and Jdate. Spark Networks SE's corporate headquarters are located in Berlin, Germany.

Each of these dating platforms seems to aim at specific demographics. Bumble appeals to users who might feel frustrated by aggressive messaging on other apps. SilverSingles focuses on adults in midlife or later. Elite Singles tends to draw professionals who prefer curated introductions.

When you look closely, you may see that each platform tells a story about who it serves. And stories, when repeated long enough, shape expectations. A person who chooses Bumble might imagine more balance between genders. These expectations may become part of the dating experience itself.

FACEBOOK DATING AND MEGA-PLATFORMS

According to Meta Platforms, Inc. (formerly Facebook, Inc.), Facebook Dating launched as an extension of the existing social media ecosystem. It allows users to create dating profiles connected to their Facebook accounts while keeping that information separate from their public feed. Some people may find comfort in the familiarity. Others might worry about privacy, which is understandable given the scale of mega-platforms.

Beyond the actual Facebook Dating, there are private Facebook groups that influence modern dating culture. Groups where women share information about potential matches. Groups where people warn each other about scammers or unhealthy patterns. These spaces might create a kind of community-based background check system. They are not formal dating platforms, but they shape how people experience dating.

One woman once told me, "I feel safer when I can look someone up in one of these groups. It tells me I am not alone." There is something genuine in that statement. A desire for community woven into the search for love. A reminder that people often want connection, but they also want safety.

NICHE AND INTERNATIONAL APPS

According to diverse market studies of global dating platforms, the digital landscape includes a wide range of niche spaces. Asian dating platforms attract users seeking cultural alignment, shared traditions, or international relationships. Faith-based apps focus on values, community ethics, and spiritual compatibility. There are also platforms built around specific lifestyles or gender preferences.

Each niche space may appear to promise something more refined than mainstream platforms. A smaller pond. A clearer sense of who is present. Yet even within these niche communities, the same human patterns appear. Hope, uncertainty, curiosity, and the desire to be seen. These spaces may provide comfort for those who feel overlooked elsewhere. They might also create new expectations that can be difficult to meet.

WHAT OWNERSHIP MEANS FOR USERS

When you understand who owns the apps, you begin to understand the environment you are walking into. Ownership shapes everything from user experience to revenue structure. It might influence how the algorithms are designed, how privacy policies are written, and how user behavior is analyzed. According to reports on digital economic trends, companies may collect data to improve matching, enhance engagement, and refine marketing strategies.

For users, this means there is always a balance to consider. Technology offers convenience and possibility. It also requires awareness. When you open an app, you enter a digital ecosystem shaped by business models, corporate priorities, and emotional patterns across millions of users. This does not make the pursuit of love less genuine. It simply means the environment has its own rules.

Closing Thought

Santiago Dagon once wrote, "The traveler who knows the terrain walks with more ease, even when the road is steep." Awareness gives you that ease. It smooths the edges. It helps you walk with calm honesty. And it reminds you that while the platforms may shape the love journey, you still decide how to walk it.

CHAPTER 3

HOW DATING APPS MAKE MONEY OFF YOUR HEART

There is an intimate reflection that happens when someone opens a dating app after a long day. The room may be dim. The air still. The smartphone glows with its blue light. A profile appears. Then another. Hope flickers. Doubt flickers too. Many people do not realize that every swipe, pause, or spark of curiosity sits inside a financial structure.

According to several digital market analyses, most dating platforms generate a significant portion of their revenue through subscriptions, data insights, and repeat user engagement. This does not mean these companies wish you harm. It simply means that love, in its digital form, lives within a business model. And understanding that model may help you move through it with more clarity and less confusion. Santiago Dagon once wrote, "Where the heart wanders, someone will build a road." Dating apps built that road. This chapter helps you see the signs along the way.

SUBSCRIPTIONS, TIERS, AND UPSELLS

The Illusion Of "Better Features = Better Matches"

Most dating apps offer free access. The invitation feels generous. You may build a profile, add a few photos, and begin to swipe. Then a message appears. It suggests that a subscription might help you meet more people. Or it may hint that upgrading could improve your visibility. According to many app store descriptions and platform disclosures, dating apps commonly use tiered subscription models that offer enhanced features such as unlimited swiping, expanded search filters, the ability to see who liked you, and access to daily boosts.

The structure may create psychological pressure. If you just pay a little more, you might find someone better. If you unlock one more feature, your chances may increase. Some people describe a sense of curiosity mixed with fear of missing out. They wonder whether they are limiting their potential by staying on the free version.

This is where compassion matters. It is human nature to reach for hope. When someone feels lonely or uncertain, a paid feature might seem like a small price for the possibility of connection. A man once told me, "I upgraded because I was tired of feeling invisible. I wanted proof that someone might see me." His honesty stayed with me. It revealed how emotionally vulnerable people become when they search for love.

The idea that a subscription directly equals better matches is not always grounded in research. It is simply part of the design. Better features may help with visibility. They do not guarantee emotional compatibility. They cannot predict chemistry. And they cannot reshape the complex truth of human connection.

PAYWALLS AROUND VISIBILITY

Boosts, Super Likes, and Algorithmic Priority.

According to publicly available platform documentation, many dating apps prioritize profiles that use paid features such as boosts or spotlight placement. These features may move a profile to the front of the line for a limited time. They may increase visibility during peak hours. They may create a sense of urgency in the user who purchases them. This type of marketing applies to many other non-dating digital platforms.

Imagine standing in a crowded room where everyone is trying to be noticed. A boost is like stepping onto a small platform for a moment. More people may see you. But it does not guarantee that the right person will stop to talk. A boost amplifies exposure, not connection.

Super Likes or enhanced interest signals work in a similar way. They may catch someone's attention. They may feel flattered. Yet they do not change who the person is or what they are seeking. They simply increase the chances that two people might begin a conversation.

People often expressed to me they felt confused by the relationship between visibility and worthiness. One woman said, "Sometimes I wonder whether the app does not show my profile unless I pay. Then I feel guilty for thinking that." Her thought reflects something many users wonder but rarely say out loud. It is not a sign of paranoia. It is a sign of how digital structures shape emotional experiences.

Apps rarely disclose the full details of their algorithms. They are not required to reveal how visibility is determined. What matters is that users understand the emotional dynamic. Increased visibility may help someone get noticed, but being noticed is not the same as being chosen for who they truly are.

DATA AS A COMMODITY

What Dating Platforms Know About You and Who They Sell It To?

According to privacy policies and public disclosures across several major platforms, dating apps often collect data such as age, location, interests, preferences, usage habits, and interaction patterns. Some platforms may also gather information about how long you look at certain profiles, which photos you dwell on, and what time of day you are most active.

Data collection is not inherently harmful. It may help dating apps improve matching accuracy, refine user experience, or detect fraudulent activity. However, the emotional weight of this information can be surprising when you think about it.

Every preference you reveal, intentionally or not, becomes part of a digital footprint.

Some platforms may share aggregated or anonymized data with third parties for marketing or research. This practice is usually disclosed in privacy agreements that many people accept without reading. The modern digital world is built on data flow. Dating apps are part of that ecosystem.

This is where a reminder may help. You are more than your data. A line of statistics cannot capture your heart integrity, your dating relationship history, the hopes you carry, or the way your voice warms up when you talk about something you enjoy. Santiago Dagon once wrote, "A soul cannot be held by numbers." Data may guide the system. It cannot define the human spirit behind the screen.

THE REVENUE OF REPETITION

Why Apps Are Not Designed for You To Leave?

According to several market research firms that study digital engagement, dating apps rely heavily on repeat activity. New sign-ups help. But returning users helps even more. This creates a financial structure where long-term user retention is beneficial. It is the architecture of most digital businesses.

If someone finds a lasting relationship, they may delete the app. If they become discouraged, they may take a break. If they feel hopeful again, they often return. The cycle may last months or years. Some people describe it as a carousel. They step off briefly, then step back on when life becomes lonely again.

One man said to me, "I have deleted this app five times. Each time I think I am done. Then a few months pass and I come back." He looked away when he said it, as if the confession carried a mixture of shame and relief. Repetition is not failure. It is simply the human longing for love meeting digital accessibility.

Apps may not be designed to encourage permanent departure. They are designed to encourage continued exploration. When you understand this rhythm, you may feel less frustration with yourself for returning, and more awareness of how these platforms are structured.

ETHICAL QUESTIONS NO ONE TALKS ABOUT

Addictive Design, Manipulative Engagement Loops, Dopamine Engineering.

According to various behavioral studies, many digital platforms use design elements that encourage repeated engagement. These can include unpredictable reward cycles, visual cues, and timed reinforcements. The experience may feel similar to social media or mobile games. A match can produce a small burst of dopamine. A message can feel like a spark. The absence of either may create a sense of longing that keeps the user checking back.

There is no accusation here. Only observation. These design choices might not be intended to manipulate. They are simply effective at keeping people engaged. Yet the emotional impact can be significant for users who are already feeling lonely, anxious, or uncertain about their romantic future.

A woman once told me, "Sometimes I know I am not looking for a date. I am just looking for a feeling. Something to remind me that I exist." Her words capture the delicate border between human vulnerability and digital reinforcement. When you understand how the loops work, you may step into the experience with more awareness and less emotional risk.

Santiago Dagon expressed it beautifully. "The flame is not the danger. The danger is forgetting that you can be burned." Awareness is the protective shield. It does not prevent hope. It simply protects the heart as it learns.

Closing Thought

As you continue reading, allow yourself to carry this understanding. Dating apps are tools. Some tools help. Some tools distract. Some tools may serve you well for a specific personal situation and then no longer fit in the life you are trying to build. The key is not to fear the online dating landscape. The key is to walk through it with open eyes and a steady guarded heart.

PART II

THE MANY FACES ON DATING APPS:

WHO YOU ARE REALLY SWIPING ON

CHAPTER 4

THE SEVEN MAJOR USER TYPES

If you sit still for a moment and picture the faces you have seen on dating apps, you may notice something subtle. They do not all belong to the same emotional world. Some appear hopeful. Some appear restless. Some seem tired in a way that is hard to name. According to several behavioral studies and survey reports on online dating patterns, users come to these platforms for many different reasons, and those reasons shape how they behave. This chapter may help you understand the emotional landscape you are walking through each time you swipe.

Santiago Dagon once wrote, "A crowd is never a single story. It is a gathering of many hearts, each carrying a different reason for arriving where they are." Dating apps reflect that truth every day.

THE SINGLE AND GENUINE SEARCHERS

Sincere Seekers, Rare but Present.

There are people on dating apps who truly want a committed relationship. They exist more than you may think. They may not be flashy. They may not have perfect profiles. Some feel nervous about putting themselves out there. Others have waited months or years before deciding to try dating again. They might adjust their photos several times, read profiles with care, and respond thoughtfully.

According to several user experience surveys, a large portion of online daters do fall into this category, though they might appear less frequently than people hope. They often get drowned out by our bias, which in fact might be totally wrong and self-sabotage our relationship search. One woman once said, "I just want to meet someone who means what they say." Her voice shook a little as she spoke, and I remember thinking how universal that desire is.

These genuine searchers may feel lost among louder personalities. Yet they are there. And they may be walking the same slow journey you are walking.

THE BORED AND LONELY

Scrolling For Validation, Entertainment, Distraction.

Late at night, the phone or the laptop screen becomes a companion. Optimism in the dark. People scroll to feel less alone. According to research on digital engagement habits, many users open dating apps when they are bored or seeking emotional stimulation rather than connection. They may not be intentionally dishonest. They may simply be lonely, unsure, or trying to fill a moment of emptiness.

A man once told me, "Sometimes I swipe because the silence in my apartment gets heavy." His honesty carried a realization that many people might relate to. These users may not intend to lead anyone on. Yet they can unintentionally create confusion because their interest appears real one day and distant the next. Boredom can mimic attraction. It can also disappear as quickly as it arrives.

THE MARRIED OR PARTNERED CHEATERS

Secret Accounts, Hidden Apps, Relationship Testing, The Thrill of Forbidden Attention.

This category may be difficult to acknowledge, yet it does exist. According to various relationship research studies, a notable number of partnered individuals use dating apps for emotional validation, secret flirtation, or sexual affairs. Some hide their apps in folders. Some create profiles under altered names. Some may claim to be separated or in "complicated situations," which might not always reflect reality.

There is often a mix of fear, desire, and avoidance behind their behavior. Some hope to test their attractiveness. Some want an escape from unmet needs. Some seek the thrill of forbidden attention.

A woman once said, "I knew he was married when he kept turning his phone upside down." Her voice carried more sadness than anger. Cheating on apps rarely begins with cruelty. It often begins with loneliness or dissatisfaction that turns into secrecy. But secrecy can harm both the cheater and the person drawn into the story. This is one of the reasons awareness matters.

THE REBOUND CROWD

Recently Hurt, Emotionally Unstable, Looking for Quick Replacement Love.

Break-ups leave a mark on the heart. According to relationship psychology research, people who enter dating apps within days or weeks of a breakup often do so in a rebound state. They may be searching for comfort. Validation. A distraction from pain.

Rebound users might come across as intense. They may fall quickly and pull away just as fast. You may feel their enthusiasm and confusion in the same breath. One person said to me, "I matched two days after my breakup. I felt seen and excited. I did not mean to hurt anyone. I just could not stand the emptiness."

Rebounds are not bad people. They are wounded people. They may promise more than they have the emotional capacity to give. They may send mixed signals without intending harm.

THE UPGRADERS

Attached But Searching for Someone "Better."

Upgraders sit in a complicated emotional space. According to several sociological studies, some people already in a relationship use apps while in the relationship, not necessarily to cheat physically but to compare. They might look for better sex, more excitement, higher social status, emotional thrill, or a fantasy that feels absent in their current life.

They may say things like, "I love my partner, but something feels missing." Or "I just want to see what else is out there." Their curiosity may appear harmless. Yet it can pull another person into a complicated triangle without warning.

Upgraders often do not recognize how much power they hold and how much harm they can do. They may draw someone in while still anchored to someone else. Santiago Dagon wrote, "When a person carries two desires, one in each hand, someone nearby will always feel the painful edge." His words feel especially true here.

THE PLAYERS AND OPPORTUNISTS

Hookup Hunters, Charm Manipulators, Emotional Predators.

Some users come to dating apps with a single goal. Casual encounters. Quick satisfaction. According to many user pattern analyses, these individuals tend to send fast messages, avoid personal questions, and move quickly toward physical suggestions.

There are also opportunists, who may enjoy emotional power. They charm. They flatter. They mirror your interests. Then they pull away once they feel they have won your attention. One person described it as "being collected and discarded."

These patterns can feel painful when you meet them unexpectedly on the dating app. But recognizing them may help you step away with clarity rather than self-blame.

THE SCAMMERS

Financial Scammers, Bots, Identity Thieves, Romance Fraud Manipulators.

Scammers represent the most dangerous edge of online dating. According to multiple global reports on cybercrime and romance fraud, financial loss, identity theft, and emotional manipulation occur on many platforms. Scammers may use stolen photos. They may craft stories that evoke sympathy. They may ask for money, personal information, or cryptocurrency.

Bots, according to several technology audits, also appear on many platforms. They may send automated messages to lure users into external websites or phishing traps.

Scammers are not seeking love. They are seeking opportunity. Awareness is your protection. And compassion toward yourself is important if you have ever fallen for a crafted illusion. Many people have become victims. Unfortunately, these victims, both male and female, are too ashamed to publicly admit their naïve mistake. These stories seldom reach the public eye.

THE INVISIBLE CATEGORY

Users Who Say They Want Love but Are Emotionally Unavailable.

This final group may be the hardest to describe. They mean well. They might believe they are ready. They may speak about commitment with sincerity. And yet something inside them remains closed.

According to psychological research on attachment, emotional unavailability can stem from fear, trauma, ambivalence, or unresolved relationships. These users may appear engaging, then pull back without warning. Or drag a relationship along for months or years without a commitment. They may crave intimacy but struggle to maintain it when it becomes real.

One man said candidly, "I want connection, but when someone gets close, I panic." He was not being cruel. He was being honest. Emotional availability is not a switch. It is a capacity.

These individuals are not villains. They are people, both male and female, in some form of transition. But they can unintentionally create heartache for those who take their early enthusiasm at face value.

Closing Thought

As you move through these categories, remember that many people shift between them based on life phase, emotion, and circumstance. You may see pieces of yourself in several sections. That is part of being human. Santiago Dagon reminds us, "Every heart is a house with many rooms. Some are well lit. Some are locked. Some open only when someone gracious arrives."

Understanding these patterns does not make dating easier. But it may help you navigate with more awareness knowing when you need to pull out of a relationship. This awareness can protect a potential broken heart and keep hope alive in the love journey ahead.

CHAPTER 5

THE HIDDEN GROUPS WITHIN PLATFORMS

There are situations on dating apps when a profile appears, and something feels slightly off. You cannot always name it. The photos seem polished. The words seem familiar. The energy feels different. Many users describe this sensation as a whispered signal in the chest or a gut feeling. A whisper that says, look more closely.

According to several behavioral studies and digital trend reports, online dating platforms often attract a range of hidden groups whose intentions may not match what most people are looking for. These groups are not always harmful. Some are simply present because dating platforms offer visibility. Others may create emotional or practical risks.

Santiago Dagon once wrote, "Every marketplace has corners that the lamps do not reach." This chapter invites you to look into those corners with awareness and a sturdy heart.

SEX WORKERS, ESCORTS, AND FETISH PROVIDERS

Why They Use Mainstream Platforms for Visibility?

According to research on digital labor and online advertising trends, some individuals working in the adult industry may use mainstream dating apps to reach potential clients or promote their services. Their profiles might feature glamorous photos, suggestive language, or ambiguous descriptions. Not all are deceptive. Some may be transparent. Others may blend into the general pool to avoid platform restrictions.

Their presence does not mean you have done anything wrong by encountering them. It simply reflects the reality that dating apps offer wide exposure. These platforms are places where people look for intimacy, which means they also attract those who sell versions of intimacy.

A man once said, "I matched with someone who looked perfect. Then the conversation changed direction. It felt like something was being offered, not shared." His words describe a common experience. This same type of comment was echoed from women being flirted by men with sneaky intentions. It may help to pause when you sense this shift. Ask yourself what you truly want. Ask whether the interaction feels mutual or transactional.

There is nothing shameful about acknowledging that some profiles serve commercial purposes. Awareness allows you to step back without confusion. Just move on forward. Dating platforms do not include disclaimers indicating that only honest and straightforward individuals are permitted.

NARCISSISTS AND VALIDATION ADDICTS

Endless Swipers Who Collect Matches Like Trophies.

There are users who come to dating apps for admiration rather than connection. According to psychological studies on digital self-esteem loops, people, both men and women, with strong validation needs may swipe endlessly to gather matches. Each match might feel like a point scored. The conversation may be brief. Sometimes it does not exist at all.

A woman told me, "He loved the attention. He loved the chase. But the moment I asked for something real, he drifted." Her reflection captures a pattern many have seen. These individuals may not intend harm. They may simply feel drawn to the quick emotional lift that digital attraction offers.

The danger lies in the imbalance. Validation addicts often take more emotional energy than they give. They may leave you feeling drained or self-critical without understanding why.

Santiago Dagon wrote, "A person who seeks only mirrors will not notice when someone offers them a window." Validation seekers often confuse reflection with connection. They are looking for themselves, not for you.

EMOTIONAL VAMPIRES

People Who Use Apps to Extract Attention, Affection, or Emotional Energy.

According to several relational behavior studies, some individuals may use dating apps to fill emotional voids rather than pursue real relationships. They may text constantly. They may ask for reassurance. They may lean on you for comfort while offering little in return.

One man said, "She told me everything about her heartbreak. Every detail. But when I needed support, she disappeared." Emotional vampires are not monsters. They are often people experiencing loneliness or unresolved personal issues. Yet their interactions can feel heavy. You may sense a slow drain of energy, even when conversations seem full of possibilities.

These connections leave a mark. You may walk away feeling tired, confused, or guilty for wanting boundaries. It is important to remember that you are allowed to protect your emotional space. Caring for someone does not require you to become their emotional reservoir.

THE "BACKUP SEEKERS"

Maintaining A Secret Roster Even When in A Relationship.

According to multiple relationship trend reports, some users maintain dating profiles while in relationships, not for active cheating but for reassurance. They may want to know options exist. They may worry about being left alone if something did happen in their current relationship. They may crave a sense of power or security.

A woman once admitted, "I never intended to meet anyone. I just liked knowing that if my relationship failed, I would not be starting from zero." Her honesty reflects the anxiety that many people carry. Backup seeking is often a symptom of fear rather than malice.

Still, this behavior can create emotional harm to those who are matched with them. You may invest time or hope into someone who has no real capacity to move forward.

Backup seekers often keep distance. Their messages may be loving but noncommittal. They may vanish when life becomes complicated, only to return weeks later with casual greetings. They treat connection as insurance, not as intimacy.

GHOSTERS, BREADCRUMBERS, AND ORBITERS

Modern Forms of Emotional Exploitation.

Digital dating created new forms of distance. According to communication research, patterns such as ghosting, breadcrumbing, and orbiting have become common vocabulary because they describe behaviors that many people experience.

Ghosting happens when someone disappears without explanation. One day the conversation is alive. The next day, silence. A man once whispered, "I thought something was wrong with me. I kept refreshing the screen." His pain was not about the person who left. It was about the sudden absence of closure.

Breadcrumbing happens when someone offers small signs of interest with no intention of moving forward. A message here. A compliment there. Enough to keep you hoping. Not enough to build anything real.

Orbiting happens when someone disengages but still watches your stories or likes your posts. They hover at the edges of your life. Close enough to remind you they exist. Too far to offer commitment.

These behaviors may appear careless rather than cruel. But they can create deep confusion. Santiago Dagon once wrote, "A half presence is still an absence. It only lingers longer." His words may help you recognize when someone offers less than your heart requires.

AI FAKE PROFILES

AI-Generated Identities Used for Romance Scams and Emotional Manipulation.

According to recent digital security reports, artificial intelligence has made it easier for scammers to create convincing fake profiles. AI-generated photos may appear realistic. Chatbots can mimic natural conversation. Scripted messages may respond instantly with warmth or curiosity.

At first glance, these profiles may seem ideal. Attractive. Polite. Interested. Yet something small may feel off. A rhythm in the conversation. A lack of deep detail. A refusal to meet on video. Scammers often use these AI-driven tools for romance fraud, identity harvesting, or phishing attempts.

One user said, "It felt like talking to a shadow. The words were there, but the person was not." His description captures the eerie sense of emptiness that sometimes appears beneath the surface of an AI-driven interaction.

Voice cloning is emerging as a powerful new tool in romance fraud. Scammers are increasingly using artificial intelligence to generate voices that align with a target's profile photo, including age, accent, and emotional tone. These synthetic voices are then used in phone or audio calls to create credibility and accelerate intimacy. Investigators note that once a victim hears a voice that feels real, skepticism drops quickly, and trust forms faster than it would through text alone. The risk is compounded by the fact that some dating platforms are simultaneously deploying AI-based voice features to enhance matchmaking, blurring the line between authentic and artificial interaction. As voice cloning technology becomes more accessible and realistic, distinguishing between genuine users and impersonators grows more difficult. This shift has raised concerns among consumer protection experts, particularly in cases where emotional dependency is leveraged to prompt financial decisions.

Awareness is essential. You do not need to mistrust everyone. You simply need to recognize when the connection feels mechanical, rehearsed, or too perfect.

Closing Thought

Remember that hidden groups exist not because people are bad, but because human needs and digital opportunity intersect in complicated ways. Many of these users are searching for something too. It may be comfort. Power. Money. Escape. Attention. Or simply reassurance that they still matter.

You are not responsible for fixing or rescuing anyone. You are only responsible for protecting your heart, your time, your money, and your emotional wellbeing. And perhaps remembering one more line from Santiago Dagon. "When you learn to see clearly, the shadows no longer frighten you. They only remind you where to place the light."

CHAPTER 6

THE REBOUNDERS, THE BROKEN, AND THE DISGUISED

There is a particular look that people carry after a break-up. The eyes glaze. The voice lowers. The shoulders seem to hold a little more weight than before. According to several psychological studies on attachment and loss, break-ups activate the same neural pathways involved in physical pain. It is one reason the heartache feels so sharp. And when a person in that tender state opens a dating app, they may not be searching for love as much as they are searching for relief.

This chapter explores the flood of rebounders that fill dating platforms, often without realizing how emotionally injured they are. Santiago Dagon once wrote, "A wounded heart does not walk. It reaches for anything that feels like a doorway." Dating apps can feel like that doorway. A bright one. A tempting one. And sometimes a costly one to those they encounter.

WHY REBOUNDERS DOMINATE

Breakup Psychology and Dopamine Seeking.

According to research published in psychological and behavioral journals, people who recently experienced break-up often show increased impulsivity, increased loneliness, and a heightened desire for distraction. Dating apps may seem like an easy place to soothe those feelings. A swipe. A match. A message. Each one releases a small burst of dopamine that might create a temporary sense of hope.

A woman once told me, "I downloaded the app the same night he left. I could not stand the silence." Her honesty reveals something important. Rebounders do not arrive with malicious intentions. They arrive because their internal world feels too emotionally heavy to carry alone.

Rebounders may dominate the digital space because break-ups happen frequently, and dating apps are always within reach. The cycle becomes self-reinforcing. Pain eases. The app provides a distraction. The distraction feels good. And somewhere in that loop, someone else unknowingly may become part of their story.

MASKING PAIN WITH ATTENTION

Why Rebounds Can Be Dangerous for Both Sides?

Rebound behavior carries a danger. Not because the wounded person is flawed, but because their heart is in transition. They are not standing on steady emotional ground. They may appear enthusiastic. They may open up quickly. They may talk about the future or share dreams that feel tender and real.

But beneath the surface there is often grief. According to relationship recovery research, unresolved pain can distort emotional judgment. The rebound user might attach too quickly. Or they might detach just as fast once the initial excitement fades.

A woman told me, "He said I made him feel alive again. Two weeks later he was gone." Her voice was mixed with confusion and disappointment. Rebound users may not intend to hurt others. They are simply trying to outrun their own sadness. And sometimes, the person who helps them forget becomes a temporary shelter rather than a partner.

The person who becomes that shelter often experiences heartbreak without understanding why. They may believe they did something wrong. They may replay conversations in their mind. They may not know that they stepped into someone else's healing process.

Rebounds are dangerous because the connection feels real. It feels intense. It feels promising. But it is often a mask worn by pain rather than a doorway into love.

THE SELF-ESTEEM CRISIS

People Using Apps to Feel Desirable Again.

According to multiple sociological studies, self-esteem often drops after a break-up. One partner may feel unwanted. The other may feel rejected or replaced. Even if the relationship ended peacefully, people may question their worth. Online attention may seem like a way to rebuild that sense of value.

A man said sincerely, "I needed someone to choose me. Anyone. Even for a moment." His words capture the vulnerability that many rebound users feel. It is not the desire for a relationship that drives them. It is the desire to feel visible seen again.

Dating apps amplify this effect. A match can act as emotional proof. A message can feel like validation. Flirtation can feel like medicine. But the relief does not last. The self-esteem boost fades quickly, which may lead someone to seek more matches, more messages, and more reassurance.

This pattern may feel harmless at first. Yet when their self-worth depends on external attention, every unanswered message feels like rejection. And every match feels like a lifeline. It can become a fragile place to search for love.

THE MIRAGE OF INSTANT CHEMISTRY

Trauma Bonding on Apps Disguised as Love.

According to several psychological analyses on attachment and trauma response, people in emotional distress often form quick and powerful bonds. This does not necessarily reflect genuine compatibility. It may reflect trauma bonding, where two painful histories temporarily align.

It may begin with long late-night conversations. Sudden vulnerability. Shared memories of heartbreak. A feeling that you have known each other forever. This intensity can feel like destiny. It might feel romantic. It could also be a sign that both people are bonding through wounds rather than through stability.

One person said to me, "We opened up so fast. It felt magical. Then everything fell apart when life got real." This is the nature of a mirage. When you move closer, the water disappears.

Trauma bonding does not mean the connection is fake. It means the connection grows faster than the emotional readiness required to sustain it. People can mistake urgency for intimacy. They can mistake intensity for compatibility. According to many relationship experts, real love grows through steadiness, not speed.

Santiago Dagon said, "A spark is honest. A flame is beautiful. But neither can warm you if there is no wood beneath." Chemistry without foundation may flicker brightly at first, then vanish without warning.

The rebounder, the broken, and the disguised are not villains in the world of online dating. They are human beings navigating emotional storms. You may have been one of them at some point. You may meet them without realizing the depth of their pain.

Closing Thought

Awareness does not require judgment. It asks only that you watch the emotional pace, listen to the tone beneath the words, and consider whether someone appears to be healing or hiding. When you understand these patterns, you may walk through the digital world with more compassion for others and more protection for yourself.

And perhaps you will hear truthfulness along the way. You deserve a connection that is not born from someone else's heartbreak. You deserve someone who meets you with a stable heart, not a wounded one searching for a bandage.

PART III

THE DARK SIDE:

DECEPTION, SCAMS, AND

MANIPULATION

CHAPTER 7

THE TRUTH ABOUT ONLINE CHEATING

There is a special kind of apprehension that settles in the stomach when someone senses that a partner might not be fully present anymore. The phone is turned face down. Messages get answered in another room. A laugh appears at the screen that does not include you. According to several relationship and technology studies, online spaces have opened new doors for forms of betrayal. Cheating has not only moved into the digital world. It has learned how to hide there.

This chapter is not written to create fear. It is written to offer language, context, and understanding, so that if you have walked near this fire, you can see its shape more clearly. Santiago Dagon once wrote, "Betrayal is not only the breaking of a promise. It is the moment one heart walks ahead while pretending to walk beside." In the world of dating apps and private messages, walking ahead can happen unnoticed and one sweep tap at a time.

HOW MANY ARE ALREADY TAKEN

The Rise of Partnered Users Seeking Secrecy.

When you open a dating app, it is natural to assume that most people are single. The idea seems reasonable. After all, these spaces are marketed as tools for "finding someone." Yet the numbers tell a more complex story.

According to research on dating app usage patterns, a sizeable portion of users report being in a committed relationship or married while using the apps. In some studies, more than half of respondents identified as partnered, even though they were active on a dating platform. Other survey work suggests that a smaller but still meaningful percentage of married or cohabiting adults use dating apps, sometimes openly in consensual arrangements, and sometimes without their partner's knowledge.

What matters here is not the exact percentage, which can vary across countries, age groups, and specific platforms. What matters is the recognition that a noticeable number of people on dating apps are not fully available. Some may be in ethically non-monogamous relationships, where all parties agree to outside connections. Others may be in traditional monogamous partnerships but still exploring in secret.

A woman once said, "He told me he was separated. But his social media showed family photos from last weekend." Her discovery is not rare. Many people learn over time that the narrative someone shares on a dating app does not always align with the life they are still living offline. A practical safeguard is to search for publicly available information about a match, not to accuse or intrude, but to protect your heart. Content visible on Google, Facebook, or social media platforms exists in the public domain. This does not mean that everyone you meet online is hiding something. It simply reflects that the digital world can make secrecy easier to maintain.

EMOTIONAL AFFAIRS IN THE DIGITAL ERA

Flirting, Sexting, Fantasy Bonds That Become Real Betrayals.

According to relationship counseling literature, emotional affairs often begin long before any physical contact. They start with small messages. A compliment. A joke. A shared confession about how "complicated" life feels. Over time, these exchanges might deepen into late-night conversations, intimate sharing, and mutual reliance that crosses the emotional boundaries of a committed relationship.

In the digital era, this process can happen very quickly. Apps and messaging platforms make it easy to stay in constant contact. Photos can be shared. Private jokes can develop. Sexting may follow. None of this requires two people to be in the same room. Yet the impact on a primary partner can be as painful as a physical affair.

People often ask, "Is it really cheating if we never met in person?" The better question might be, "Would I feel betrayed if my partner did this with someone else?" Many spouses and partners report that discovering intimate messages or ongoing digital flirtations felt like a deep breach of trust, even if there was no physical contact.

A man once told me, "She kept saying it was just talking. But she told him things she never tells me." His voice carried more hurt than anger. It was not the messages alone that wounded him. It was the shift in intimacy. Emotional affairs relocate closeness. They take something that belongs in one relationship and move it into another.

Santiago Dagon wrote, "The heart knows when it has been replaced, even if no one has moved out of the house." Emotional cheating might never leave a physical mark, but it often leaves an invisible scar.

MARRIED AND USING DATING APPS: WHY?

Escape, Validation, Midlife Crisis, Sexual Boredom, Ego Insecurity.

When people in long-term relationships create profiles on dating apps, the reasons are rarely simple. According to various studies and clinical observations from therapists, common motives include emotional escape, the search for validation, midlife crisis experiences, sexual dissatisfaction, curiosity, and underlying insecurity about aging or desirability.

Some individuals describe feeling invisible at home. Others speak about years of unresolved conflict. Some mention the fear that life is passing by. They may say things like, "I just wanted to see if I still had it." Or "I was not really going to meet anyone. I just wanted to feel wanted."

These reasons do not excuse betrayal, but they help explain how it begins. Online spaces offer quick rewards. A match or flirty message can ease the feelings of rejection or boredom for a moment. According to research on digital reinforcement, these small bursts of attention may function like emotional painkillers. They do not heal the marriage. They temporarily numb discomfort.

There is also the practical reality that dating apps are always available. They reside on the smartphone 24/7, waiting. A partner does not need to leave the house to cheat. They only need a spare moment in the kitchen, a late night in the living room, or a drive in a parked car.

When we look at these behaviors through a compassionate but honest lens, we might say that many married users on apps are not primarily looking for a new life. They are looking for a new feeling. The danger is that, in chasing that feeling, they can fracture the trust that holds their existing life together.

THE "UPGRADE MENTALITY"

Relationship Comparison and Constant Dissatisfaction.

There is a mindset that online dating can encourage partner dissatisfaction, even for people who are already in a serious monogamous relationship. It might sound like this. "What if there is someone slightly more attractive? Slightly more exciting? Slightly better suited to me?" This is the upgrade mentality. It frames relationships like devices. Version 1.0, 2.0, 3.0. According to some social psychology research, environments with many visible options can increase dissatisfaction with existing choices, even if those choices are objectively good.

Dating apps display people, the way online shops highlight their products. New faces appear every time you swipe. Profiles highlight the best angles. It becomes easy to forget that every person is a complex human being, not a collection of features. When someone who is already in a relationship spends time on these platforms, they may begin to compare. Their partner's flaws stand out next to a stranger's polished profile. The comparison is not fair, but it can feel very real.

A man in a long-term relationship said, "I love my partner, but the app showed me so many other types of women. It made me question everything." He did not sound proud of this. He sounded unsettled. The upgrade mentality does not create peace. It creates permanent second-guessing.

For the person who is single and serious about connection, meeting someone with an upgrade mindset can be deeply painful. You may be treated like an experiment. A test run. If something feels slightly off, they may return to the app without saying much, convinced that a more perfect match is just one more swipe away.

Santiago Dagon offers a reality check. "Love is not about finding the best possible person. It is about becoming the most honest possible self with someone who is willing to do the same." Upgrading devices makes sense in consumer culture.

Upgrading people does not. It turns partners into objects, and relationships into temporary contracts.

Closing Thought

As you reflect upon this chapter, notice any memories or feelings that surface. Perhaps you have been on the receiving end of digital cheating. Perhaps, at some point in your life, you have been the one scrolling in secret, trying to ease an ache you did not know how to name. This is not about shame. It is about understanding.

When you see how online cheating really works, you gain the ability to choose differently. To ask for honesty. To offer it. To protect your heart without hardening it. And to remember that while apps can tempt people into hidden paths, they cannot force anyone to walk them.

The decision to be faithful, in both body and heart, still lives in the choices each person makes when the screen lights up and no one else is watching.

CHAPTER 8

THE SCAM INDUSTRY BEHIND DATING APPS

There is a disclosure in many dating conversations when a person lowers their voice and says, "I never thought it would happen to me." The shock of being deceived online carries a special sting. It touches both the heart and the pride.

According to multiple international cybercrime and consumer protection reports, romance scams and identity-based fraud have grown significantly over the past decade. Dating apps did not create these dangers, but they have become common places where scammers search for vulnerable targets.

This chapter is not meant to frighten you. It is meant to educate you. When you understand how these scams work, you may feel less ashamed if you have ever been fooled, and more prepared if someone tries to fool you. Santiago Dagon once wrote, "A trusting heart is not a weakness. It is a sign of life. The danger is not in trusting. The danger is in trusting without seeing."

ROMANCE SCAMS

Scripts, Methods, Emotional Manipulation, Common Storylines.

According to consumer protection agencies across several countries, romance scams are among the most financially damaging forms of online fraud. Scammers often follow predictable scripts. They begin with flattery. Affection. Quick emotional bonding. They might tell you that you are special. You are meant for them. Destined, even. Some claim to be overseas for work. Some say they are widowed. Some describe tragic hardships that seem designed to pull at compassion.

A common pattern appears in the speed of emotional intimacy. A scammer may say "I love you" early. They may ask for exclusivity. They may send long messages filled with tender phrases. The goal is to create a fantasy bond strong enough to make the victim overlook red flags.

After the emotional hook is secure, the story shifts. A crisis appears. Medical bills. Travel problems. Business emergencies. Frozen bank accounts. They ask for help. Sometimes small amounts. Sometimes large. The story changes as needed to maintain pressure.

One woman said, "He made me believe I was saving him. I only realized later that I was saving a ghost." Her reflection is shared by many people worldwide. It is not foolishness that traps victims. It is empathy. It is loneliness. It is the human desire to be needed.

IDENTITY THEFT OPERATIONS

Phishing, data harvesting, fake profiles, synthetic personas.

According to multiple cybersecurity reports, identity thieves use dating platforms to collect personal information. They may ask innocent-seeming questions. Where do you work? Where do you bank? The city you grew up in? They may steer conversations toward photos that reveal addresses, license plates, or workplace locations. Some send links that appear friendly but are designed to capture passwords or install malicious software.

Fake profiles often include stolen photos. These images may belong to real people who have no idea their likeness is being used. The scammer builds a synthetic identity. A blend of truth and fiction. A character designed to feel trustworthy.

A man once told me, "She knew details about me that I did not remember sharing. That was when fear replaced excitement." Identity-based scams rely on subtlety. They move slowly. They use charm as a tool. Protecting yourself does not require paranoia. It requires awareness. Never share personal information too quickly. Never click unknown links. And trust your instinct gut feeling when something feels too polished.

THE BOT EPIDEMIC

AI-Generated Profiles That Imitate Human Conversation.

According to technology analysts, artificial intelligence has allowed scammers to create highly realistic fake accounts. AI-generated images can look shockingly real. Chatbots can respond with rehearsed tender phrases and appropriate timing. Some can mimic humor. Some can mirror your tone.

At first, the conversation may seem ideal. The person responds quickly. They rarely challenge you. They compliment everything you say. Yet something feels slightly off. The rhythm is too smooth. The stories are vague. The emotions feel copied, not lived.

A user once said, "It felt like speaking with a shadow that knew how to smile." His words capture the uncanny nature of AI-driven deception.

Bots are often used to pull people into external scams. They may direct you to subscription websites. Or cryptocurrency schemes. Or fake investment platforms. They pretend to care. But they only care about the next step in the trap.

When the person on the screen feels perfect, take a moment to pause. Perfection is rarely human.

FINANCIAL FRAUD RINGS

Organized Criminal Networks Posing as Lovers.

According to international law enforcement and cybersecurity investigations, some romance scams are not run by individuals but by coordinated groups. These operations may involve teams who create profiles, write scripts, handle money, and train new recruits. Their methods are professional. Their emotional manipulation is practiced. Their communication patterns are structured like a job, not a relationship.

These fraud rings often target people who appear financially stable or emotionally vulnerable. The recently widowed is a prime target sourced public obituary notices. They might attempt to move conversations off the platform quickly. They may pressure victims to invest in fake business opportunities. Some may build a relationship over months and sometimes over years before asking for money.

A sad unseen tragedy unfolds here. Many victims do not report these crimes because they feel ashamed. They fear judgment. They fear people will ask how they could have believed the lies. Yet according to major fraud prevention organizations, victims span every age group, every income bracket, and every level of education.

Loneliness is not a lack of intelligence. It is a human condition.

HOW MUCH MONEY IS LOST EVERY YEAR

Investigated Numbers: Billions Globally.

According to consumer protection agencies and international fraud reports, financial losses from romance scams reach billions of dollars globally each year. Some countries track these numbers closely. Others struggle because many victims never come forward. The emotional cost, which cannot be measured, is often far greater than the money lost.

People describe a grief that feels deeper than financial betrayal. They grieve the imagined future. The messages. The affection shown. The belief that someone finally saw them.

One man said, "I did not lose money. I lost a version of myself." His words reveal the real wound behind these crimes.

Santiago Dagon wrote, "It is not the thief who breaks the heart. It is the moment you realize the love you held was only your own reflection." This truth may feel heavy. Yet seeing it clearly is part of healing.

Closing Thought

This chapter may unsettle you. Many people feel a chill when they learn how wide the scam industry has grown. Yet fear is not the goal. Awareness is. When you can name the shadows, they lose much of their power. And when you walk through the digital world with eyes open, you give yourself the gift of safety without losing the possibility of connection.

You do not need to trust everyone. You only need to trust yourself enough to listen when something doesn't feel right. The heart is wiser than we give it credit for.

CHAPTER 9

SPOTTING THE CROOKED, THE DANGEROUS, AND THE TOXIC

There is a small flash inside most dating conversations when something feels slightly illogical. A pause that stretches too long. A compliment that lands too heavy. A story that bends in a direction that does not quite make sense. Many people ignore these split-second gut feelings because the desire for connection feels stronger than the discomfort. Yet according to many psychological and cybersecurity studies, early red flags often appear long before the danger becomes clear.

This chapter is not written to create suspicion. It is written to help you trust your instincts. Santiago Dagon once wrote, "A whisper of doubt is the heart trying to protect its future." When you learn to listen to those whispers, you may walk through the digital world with far greater safety.

THE MICRO-RED FLAGS

Timing, Messaging Patterns, Evasive Behaviors.

Micro-red flags are small signals. Easy to overlook. Easy to explain away. They may appear harmless at first, but they often reveal a deeper pattern. Below are some examples:

Inconsistent Timing.

A person who always messages late at night and avoids daytime communication might be hiding something. They may have another relationship. They may live in a different time zone than they claim. They might prefer secrecy.

Rapid Intimacy.

Someone who calls you darling or baby in the first few exchanges may seem affectionate. But many scammers and manipulative personalities use fast intimacy to create emotional attachment before trust is earned.

Avoidance Of Simple Questions.

If you ask something basic, such as "What part of the city are you in?" and the answer shifts into a story rather than a location, notice that. Evasion is a warning.

Uneven Conversation.

A user who sends long paragraphs but never answers your questions may not be having a real dialogue. They may be copy-pasting scripts. Or they may not care enough to engage fully.

Last-Minute Cancellations.

People who repeatedly cancel plans right before meeting may be hiding their real identity or struggling with honesty.

A woman once said, "Every time we planned to meet, he had an excuse. I wanted to believe him. I tried. But my chest felt tight each time. It knew the truth before I did." Sometimes the heart reads signs faster than the mind.

THE MACRO-RED FLAGS

Lies, Inconsistencies, Unfair Demands, Emotional Manipulation.

Macro-red flags are harder to deny. They may appear after a few days or a few weeks, and they often indicate that something dangerous or unhealthy is unfolding. Below are some examples:

Inconsistencies In Their Story.

Someone might say they live in one city, then later mention a completely different one. They might claim to be a certain age, but their timeline does not add up. According to several fraud analyses, inconsistencies are one of the strongest predictors of deception.

Unwillingness To Video Chat.

Many scammers refuse live video. People with double lives may avoid it too. A simple video call can reveal more truth than weeks of messages.

Pressure To Move Fast.

If someone pushes you into commitment within days or says you are the person they have waited for without knowing you, pause. Love does not require haste.

Emotional Manipulation.

Statements like "If you cared you would do this" or "I guess you are not as loyal as I thought" are signals of future emotional abuse. These interactions might escalate over time.

Financial Requests or Emergencies.

Any request for money, cryptocurrency, gift cards, or help with travel arrangements is a bright red warning. According to numerous consumer protection agencies, financial requests are one of the clearest signs of a romance scam.

Macro-red flags require courage to face. They test your willingness to prioritize your safety over your hopes. Maintain Awareness. Think. When it feels unusual or too good to be true, maybe it is!

SCAMMER DETECTION TECHNIQUES

Reverse Image Search, Conversation Traps, Behavioral Tests.

There are practical techniques you can use to protect yourself against scammers. Below are some examples:

Reverse Image Search.

According to cybersecurity guidance, using a reverse image search tool can reveal whether a profile photo appears on other websites. If you find the same face attached to different names or locations, the profile may be fake.

Ask Specific Questions.

Scammers often struggle with details. Ask about small local places, current weather, sports teams, recent news, or restaurant references that require real familiarity. A vague or confused answer might reveal something.

Watch For Language Patterns.

Many scam messages have a similar tone. Overly formal. Strangely poetic. Slightly out of rhythm with casual conversation. If every message feels like a script, it might be one.

Request A Quick Video Call.

A genuine person might feel shy but usually agrees after a bit of trust forms. Refusal to appear on camera is a significant warning sign.

Change The Subject Suddenly.

Scammers often follow training scripts. If you shift the topic abruptly, they may respond in mismatched or odd ways.

A man once smiled and told me, "I asked her what her favorite pizza place was?" She answered with a long speech about destiny." He laughed softly. But beneath the humor there was relief. He had avoided something painful.

WHEN TO WALK AWAY IMMEDIATELY

Non-Negotiables That Protect Your Safety and Sanity.

There are instances when hesitation is dangerous. If any of these occur, you should walk away without explanation, without guilt, and without looking back. Below are some examples:

Requests For Money of Any Kind.

It might be disguised as a business emergency, a family crisis, or travel complications. It does not matter. It is a clear exit point.

Refusal To Meet in Person After Reasonable Time.

Online connection cannot replace real presence. Endless excuses suggest deception or emotional unavailability.

Verbal Aggression, Guilt Trips, Or Pressure.

Small displays of disrespect or overly affectionate suggestions early on hint at future harm.

Contradictory Information About Identity.

If the story changes, trust the red flag, not the excuse.

You Feel Unsafe or Unsettled.

Your instinct is one of your strongest protective tools. According to many trauma and psychological studies, people often sense danger before they can articulate it.

Santiago Dagon wrote, "It is not unkind to protect yourself. It is a form of wisdom." Leaving early can be an act of deep self-respect.

CASE STUDIES OF REAL VICTIMS

Anonymous Stories to Illustrate Patterns.

These stories are fictional composites based on common patterns reported in public scam data and counseling experiences. No single person is represented. They are meant to illustrate how easily good people can be caught in painful experiences.

Case Study One: The Sudden Soldier.

Maria met a man who claimed to be deployed overseas. He messaged daily with affection. After two weeks, he said he wanted to build a life with her. Then came the request. His bank account was frozen. He needed a small loan to return home. She sent it. Months passed. She discovered the photos belonged to a real soldier who had no idea his image was being used.

Case Study Two: The Perfect Match.

Derrick connected with someone who seemed ideal. Same hobbies. Same humor. Same dreams. The profile was flawless. Almost too flawless. When Derrick asked for a video call, the excuses began. A broken camera. A lost phone. A work emergency. He later learned through a reverse image search that the photos were AI generated.

Case Study Three: The Emotional Drain.

Lena spent weeks supporting a man who said he was struggling with depression. She shared resources and listened to his fears. But whenever she needed support, he withdrew. Eventually she realized he was contacting several women at the same time, drawing emotional energy from each without offering anything back.

Each story carries a theme. Trust misplaced. Hope exploited. Courage required to move forward.

Closing Thought

As you reach the end of this chapter, take a breath. You may feel a mixture of caution and clarity. That is natural. You are not meant to fear every interaction. You are meant to recognize when something does not feel right and respond with confidence rather than confusion.

Your heart is worthy of protection. And you are allowed to walk away the moment something feels crooked. Santiago Dagon reminds us, "Wisdom is not knowing who to trust. Wisdom is knowing when to stop giving trust away."

PART IV

THE APPS THEMSELVES:

WHAT THEY PROMISE VS. WHAT THEY DELIVER

CHAPTER 10

TINDER: THE ILLUSION OF ENDLESS OPTIONS

There is a distinctive sensation that arises the first time someone opens Tinder. The screen lights up. A face appears. Then another. Then another. It feels like standing in front of an endless parade of possibilities. Many users describe a strange excitement mixed with a strange emptiness.

According to several psychological studies on digital choice environments, the human mind is not built for limitless options. It becomes overwhelmed, overstimulated, and sometimes desensitized. Tinder's design intensifies this by inviting you to swipe quickly rather than reflect deeply.

This chapter is not meant to criticize Tinder. Tinder, like other dating apps, are not harmful. This chapter is meant to help you understand what the app is, what it is not, and how you can use it without losing your sense of self. Santiago Dagon once wrote, "Too many doors can make a person forget what they came searching for." Tinder offers many doors. The real question is whether the doorway leads you toward connection or distraction.

IS TINDER DESIGNED FOR A LASTING CONNECTION?

The Psychological Impact of Infinite Choice.

According to several behavioral and relationship studies, Tinder was originally designed as a quick interface for mutual attraction, not long-term compatibility. Its swipe structure prioritizes immediate interest, physical appeal, and rapid decision making. The app does not ask about values, life goals, or emotional readiness. It simply asks whether you like what you see.

This might seem fun. But when people scroll through hundreds of profiles in a short time, the brain begins to treat human beings like interchangeable items. The psychological term often used to describe this is "Choice Overload." When options become too numerous, people may make poorer decisions or avoid decisions altogether.

A man once said to me, "Every time I matched with someone, I thought, what if someone better appears the next minute?" His honesty reflects a pattern seen in many users. Too many possibilities may create restlessness rather than commitment.

Santiago Dagon explained this feeling in a single line: "Abundance without purpose becomes a kind of hunger." Dating apps can feed that hunger without ever satisfying it.

HOOKUP CULTURE AND THE ATTENTION ECONOMY

Do Sweep Apps Thrives on Superficiality?

According to consumer experiences, Tinder is widely associated with casual encounters. This does not mean everyone uses it for that purpose. Many sincere individuals are on Tinder. Some even find long-term partners. However, the structure of the app leans toward quick attraction. Fast conversation. Minimal emotional investment.

The swipe app operates within the attention economy. The more user swipe, the more they engage with premium features, boosts, and visibility upgrades. Quick profiles and brief interactions keep people active. The app appears to reward faces, poses, and aesthetics more than depth. This can create a culture where people feel pressure to present highly curated versions of themselves.

A woman shared, "I felt like I had to become a highlight reel, not a person." Her words hold truth for many. The app encourages surface judgments. This is not immoral. It is simply the nature of the platform.

Tinder, like most dating apps, thrives when people keep returning. When connections are short-lived. When curiosity remains unsatisfied. Dating apps do not promise long-term connection. The promise possibility. Those are two very different things.

CHEATERS, PLAYERS, AND ADDICTIVE SWIPING LOOPS

Behavioral Insights.

According to multiple user behavior analyses, Tinder, like most dating apps, attract a diverse range of personalities. Many are kind, respectful, and genuinely searching. Others include players, serial daters, married individuals seeking secrecy, or thrill seekers. The very structure of the swipe app creates conditions where these behaviors flourish. Below ae some examples:

Rapid Swiping Encourages Detachment.

When a decision takes less than a second, empathy may lessen. People become profiles rather than individuals. It becomes easier to ghost, breadcrumb, or juggle multiple conversations.

Cheaters Find Cover in the Swipe Design.

The swipe design allows quick cycles of matching and unmatching. A person who is in a relationship can use the app silently for validation or secret excitement without leaving a long digital trail.

Addictive Loops Emerge.

According to research on dopamine reinforcement, the unpredictable reward of matches can create a slot-machine effect. Swipe after swipe. A match. A rush. Another swipe. Another small surge.

One man confessed, "Sometimes I went on the app even when I did not want to meet anyone. I just wanted the feeling of being chosen." His confession reflects something many users feel privately. Tinder swiping can become an emotional vending machine. But like most vending machines, the nourishment may be temporary.

Santiago Dagon wrote, "The thrill of being noticed is not the same as the peace of being known." Tinder often offers the first being noticed. It may take effort to reach the second.

TINDER: THE POSITIVE SIDE

A List of Genuine Strengths and Why Tinder Might Be Good for You.

Despite its limitations, Tinder is not inherently harmful. Used with awareness, it can be a helpful tool. Many people have met partners, built friendships, and regained confidence through the app. Below are some positive qualities of Tinder:

1. Large User Base.

According to public usage reports, Tinder has millions of active users worldwide, which increases the chances of meeting diverse people.

2. Ease Of Use.

The interface is simple. No long questionnaires. No complicated setup. It works for people who prefer fast, visual introductions.

3. Useful For Boosting Social Confidence.

For individuals returning to dating after a breakup or long pause, Tinder can help ease them into conversations and rebuild self-esteem.

4. Good For Exploring Your Type.

Seeing numerous profiles may help you learn what you are drawn to and what you do not want.

5. Allows Casual Interactions Without Pressure.

Some people do not want a relationship immediately. Tinder may serve as a safe place to meet new faces without heavy commitment.

6. Can Lead To Real Relationships.

While Tinder is not optimized for long-term matching, many couples have met there forming long-term relationships.

TINDER MIGHT SERVE YOU WELL IF:

- You enjoy meeting new people casually.

- You prefer visual first impressions.

- You are exploring what you want romantically.

- You need a low-pressure way to ease back into dating.

- You want to practice communication in a relaxed environment.

- You are comfortable navigating a fast-paced, high-choice platform.

Tinder is simply a dating connection tool. The question is whether the tool aligns with your emotional needs at this moment in your life.

Santiago Dagon reminds us gently, "A compass cannot choose your direction. It only shows where you stand." Tinder is a compass of sorts. It offers path of possibilities. Faces that come and go. You decide which direction you choose to walk.

If you walk with awareness, you may find moments of real connection in a sea of noise. If you walk blindly, the noise may overwhelm you. The power, as always, is in the way you move through the world, not the world itself.

CHAPTER 11

BUMBLE, HINGE, MATCH, AND THE "RELATIONSHIP APPS"

There is a sense of hope in the moment someone shifts from a fast-swipe app to one marketed for relationships. The heart leans forward. The breath deepens. It feels like stepping out of a crowded street and into a calmer neighborhood where people walk a little slower and speak with more intention.

According to several industry and user experience studies, apps like Bumble, Hinge, Match, and SilverSingles attract individuals who say they want something more stable. But the truth, as always, is more layered. Motives vary. Behaviors vary. Outcomes vary.

Still, many users feel that these platforms offer a more grounded environment than purely swipe-based spaces. Santiago Dagon once wrote, "The place we choose to search shapes the way we learn to love." Each of these apps creates a different emotional landscape. Understanding those landscapes may help you walk with more wisdom.

BUMBLE: EMPOWERMENT OR STILL ANOTHER SWIPE APP?

Women Message First, But Motives Still Mixed.

According to Bumble's public mission statements, the platform was designed to give women more control by requiring them to send the first message after a match. This shift may reduce certain types of unwanted messages. It may create a sense of empowerment for women who feel tired of being approached aggressively on other platforms.

However, Bumble still relies heavily on swiping, which means fast judgment, visual emphasis, and the addictive scroll remain part of the experience. Men may feel uncertain about how much to initiate. Women may feel pressure to start conversations even when they are unsure. Several users report that the "women message first" rule can feel powerful in theory, but uneven in practice.

A woman once said, "I liked the control, but I still had trouble finding sincerity. It felt like Tinder in nicer clothing." Another said, "Bumble helped me feel safer. That alone made it worth trying." Both realities may be true at the same time.

The motives of Bumble users vary widely. Some seek long-term relationships. Some seek casual encounters. Some seek entertainment or validation. Bumble tries to shape the culture. But people bring their own stories, wounds, habits, and hopes into the Bumble space.

HINGE: "DESIGNED TO BE DELETED?"

Marketing Promise vs. Actual Outcomes.

According to Hinge's public branding, the platform is "designed to be deleted," positioning itself as the relationship-focused alternative to swipe apps. Hinge encourages longer profiles, conversation prompts, and more thoughtful exchanges. The design slows users down just enough to create space for personality.

Yet outcomes may differ. Some users report meaningful connections and long-term relationships. Others describe ghosting, breadcrumbing, and the same emotional turbulence seen elsewhere. A man once told me, "Hinge felt like people wanted something serious until they did not." His tone carried a mixture of hope and fatigue.

Hinge does create opportunities for deeper engagement. But depth requires two people willing to meet each other honestly. The app cannot create that willingness. It only provides the framework. Sincerity has to come from the people using it. Santiago Dagon's words fit well here: "A path can guide your steps. It cannot choose the direction of your heart."

MATCH.COM AND EHARMONY

Legacy Platforms, Compatibility Systems, Mixed Demographics.

Match.com and eHarmony remain two of the most established dating platforms. They emerged before the swipe era and focused more heavily on profiles, search filters, and compatibility questionnaires.

Match.com

Match feels broad and inclusive. It draws users from many age groups, especially adults in their thirties and older who want something more stable and are comfortable with a slower, more traditional format.

eHarmony

eHarmony emphasizes compatibility with algorithms. The platform uses detailed questionnaires and personality frameworks to match users. Many older adults and divorced individuals gravitate toward it because it feels structured, calm, and less focused on appearances.

Both Match.com and eHarmony platforms tend to attract people who are serious about relationships. But seriousness does not guarantee alignment. Some join out of loneliness. Others join out of pressure from friends or family. And some join out of vulnerability after a loss.

Still, these legacy platforms may offer a less chaotic environment with fewer impulsive interactions.

SILVERSINGLES AND NICHE SENIOR APPS

Older Adults, Companionship Seekers, Vulnerability to Scams.

Senior dating platforms such as SilverSingles, OurTime, and other niche apps attract adults aged fifty and above who seek companionship, emotional support, and sometimes romance after divorce or widowhood. These platforms can be meaningful spaces for people who want to share life with someone new in a later chapter.

However, research from multiple consumer protection agencies suggests that older adults may be more vulnerable to certain types of scams. Loneliness, grief, and trust can open doors for manipulative profiles. Scammers often target these individuals because they know users may be searching for comfort, stability, or emotional closeness. It should be noted, dating platforms have security to help eliminate the scammer threat.

A widower shared, "I joined because the nights felt too alone. I just wanted someone to talk to." His reflection captures the emotional landscape of these platforms. They hold great promise for healing connection. They also require careful attention to red flags.

THE POSITIVE QUALITIES OF BUMBLE, HINGE, MATCH.COM, AND SILVERSINGLES

Why They Might Be Good for You?

Each app has genuine strengths. The key is to match the dating platform with your emotional needs, your stage of life, and your relationship goals.

Bumble - Positive Qualities

1. Women initiate the first message, which may reduce inappropriate contact.

2. Encourages respectful communication.

3. Simple interface.

4. Good balance between casual and serious dating.

5. Attractive to young professionals who want a safer environment.

Why Bumble Might Be Good for You?

You might thrive on Bumble if you appreciate empowerment, want more control over interactions, or prefer an environment that discourages aggressive approaches.

HINGE - Positive Qualities

1. Thoughtful prompts encourage real conversation.

2. Profiles reveal personality beyond photos.

3. Slower pace than swipe-heavy apps.

4. Attracts users seeking relationships.

5. Designed to encourage meaningful interactions.

Why HINGE Might Be Good for You?

You may enjoy Hinge if you value conversation, emotional depth, and a platform that tries to reduce superficiality.

Match.com - Positive Qualities

1. Large, long-established user base.

2. Comprehensive profiles.

3. Strong search filters.

4. Popular among people seeking commitment.

5. Offers more structure for intentional dating.

Why Match Might Be Good for You?

Match may suit you if you want a traditional experience and enjoy the stability of a platform that has existed for decades.

eHarmony - Positive Qualities

1.   Extensive compatibility matching.

2.   Deep questionnaires to identify values.

3.   Attracts commitment-oriented adults.

4.   Less emphasis on swiping culture.

5.   Good for people who prefer structure and slower pacing.

Why eHarmony Might Be Good for You?

This platform may help you if you want a relationship built on shared values and long-term compatibility.

SilverSingles and Senior Apps - Positive Qualities

1.   Designed for adults over fifty.

2.   Emphasis on companionship and emotional support.

3.   Matches based on stability, shared lifestyles, and similar life stages.

4.   A respectful environment with less superficial pressure.

5.   Many users seek genuine long-term partnership.

Why Senior Apps Might Be Good for You?

These spaces may be healing if you want connection after loss, want slower emotional pacing, or prefer dating with peers who understand your life stage.

Closing Thought

As you reflect upon this chapter, notice what resonates. You may feel hope, or the caution of experience. Both are natural. Santiago Dagon reminds us, "The right place does not guarantee love. It simply helps the heart breathe more easily."

Choose the app that allows your heart to breathe. The rest will unfold with time, honesty, and awareness.

CHAPTER 12

OKCUPID, POF, FACEBOOK DATING, AND FREE PLATFORMS

There is a positive comfort in the word "Free." It can feel like low risk. Low pressure. A way to dip a toe into the dating world without making a financial commitment. Many people start with free platforms for that reason. According to the public descriptions on each service, apps like OkCupid, Plenty of Fish (POF), and Facebook Dating try to offer connection without a paywall at the front door. Yet, as with most things in life, Free does not necessarily mean simple.

In this chapter, we will walk through some of the more open, less structured corners of online dating. These places can hold real possibility. They can also feel chaotic. Santiago Dagon once wrote, "A field without fences grows wild. Beauty appears there, and thorns as well." Free platforms often feel like that field.

OKCUPID: VALUES-BASED OR CHAOS-BASED?

Questionnaires vs. Reality.

The OkCupid platform tends to focus on questions and compatibility. Users answer prompts about politics, religion, habits, and preferences. The app then uses those answers to show a match percentage, suggesting how closely two people may align in beliefs or lifestyle. On the surface, this seems like a thoughtful approach. It invites people to think beyond looks.

In practice, the experience can be mixed. Some users take the questions seriously. They sit at their desk, coffee beside them, and answer as honestly as they can. Others skip through quickly or treat the questions as entertainment. The result is a space that might feel deeply value-based one moment and somewhat chaotic the next.

A man once told me, "I liked seeing where we matched and where we did not. It helped me ask better questions on dates." A women said, "The percentages looked great, but the reality felt different." Both experiences are true. Numbers can guide, but they cannot fully capture human complexity.

OkCupid's strength lies in its attempt to look beneath the surface. However, people still choose how seriously they engage with that structure.

OkCupid - Positive Qualities

1. **Values-based matching.** The question system encourages reflection on beliefs, habits, and priorities.

2. **Room for nuance.** Profiles can show more than photos. They can reveal humor, intellect, and worldview.

3. **Flexible settings.** Users can explore different types of connections, from casual to serious.

4. **Good for introspection.** Answering questions may clarify what truly matters to you.

Why OkCupid Might Be Good for You?

OkCupid may fit you if you care about alignment on issues such as politics, spirituality, lifestyle, and social values, and if you enjoy deeper profiles rather than quick swipes.

PLENTY OF FISH: THE WILD WEST

High Volume, Low Accountability.

The Plenty of Fish (POF) platform has long been positioned as a large, free, open dating site with a very broad user base. Many people describe it as busy, crowded, and unpredictable. New profiles appear constantly. Messages can arrive quickly and in high volume, especially for women.

Because the platform is open and widely accessible at little to no cost, it may attract a wide spectrum of intentions. Serious daters. Casual browsers. Lonely people. Opportunists. Scammers. Everything can mingle together. Some users feel that there is less accountability because creating a profile is easy and walking away is easier.

A woman said, "POF felt like a noisy bar. There were good people there. But I had to look hard to find them." Her metaphor is accurate for many. For certain personalities, the high volume may feel exciting. For others, it may feel overwhelming.

The "Wild West" feeling is not the fault of the platform alone. It is what happens when many different human stories share one large, loose space.

Plenty Of Fish (POF) - Positive Qualities

1. **Large, diverse user base.** Many people in many regions, which can increase your chances of finding someone nearby.

2. **Completely free core features.** You can message and interact without paying.

3. **Good for practice.** The high volume of interaction can help you practice boundaries, conversation skills, and discernment.

4. **Useful for casual exploration.** You can see a broad cross-section of personalities and intentions.

Why POF Might Be Good for You?

Plenty of Fish might suit you if you are patient, willing to filter through noise, and interested in meeting many different types of people without financial investment.

FACEBOOK DATING AND FACEBOOK GROUPS

Are We Dating the Same Guy?

Facebook Dating is an optional feature within the larger Facebook ecosystem. It allows users to create separate dating profiles while still drawing from their existing network and interests. For some people, this feels safer. Familiar. They feel reassured by seeing mutual friends or shared communities.

At the same time, Facebook has become home to private vetting groups such as versions of "Are We Dating the Same Guy?" where women in particular share information about dating experiences, red flags, and concerns. These groups do not exist to attack individuals. They exist to protect members from repeated patterns of deception, dishonesty, or manipulation.

When someone says, "I searched his name in the group and saw three posts about him," the mood shifts. These community spaces reveal how common certain behaviors have become. Ghosting. Overlapping relationships. Hidden marriages. Emotional abuse. They also show the power of shared knowledge. A pattern that might be invisible to one person becomes clear when several stories align.

Facebook Dating itself may work well for people whose social lives are already anchored in that platform. The surrounding groups show that modern daters are no longer alone in their experiences. They can compare notes. They can warn each other. They can support each other after difficult encounters.

Facebook Dating and Facebook Groups - Positive Qualities

1. **Integrated with your existing life.** Shared friends and communities can provide context.

2. **Safer feeling for some users.** Seeing mutual connections may feel more grounding.

3. **Community vetting.** Groups like "Are We Dating The Same Guy?" and similar communities can offer protection, perspective, and support.

4. **Organic connection.** Friendship and interest groups allow relationships to grow from shared activities rather than pure attraction.

Why Facebook Dating and Groups Might Be Good for You?

These spaces may work well if you like meeting people through mutual circles, want some social context around new matches, or feel more comfortable in community-based environments than in anonymous apps.

FRIENDSHIP AND INTEREST GROUPS

How Did These Groups Accidentally Become Dating Pools of Their Own?

Outside of formal dating features, there are countless friendships and interest groups that have turned into dating pools. According to observations from social media researchers, hobby communities, local discussion groups, and spiritual or wellness circles on platforms like Facebook or Meetup often become places where romantic connection begins.

People join for shared interests. Hiking. Books. Parenting. Grief support. Creativity. Over time, friendships form. Private messages begin. A conversation about a book becomes a conversation about life. Then two people meet for coffee. No formal dating app was involved, yet the digital space still acted as a bridge.

A man said, "I met her in a meditation group. Neither of us was looking for love. It just happened." Stories like this suggest that when people gather around something meaningful, relationships may grow more naturally.

The upside is that there are often more context and accountability. Mutual friends may know both parties. The downside is that when a romance fails, the shared group can become awkward. Yet these spaces remain important alternatives for those who feel exhausted by formal dating platforms.

Free Platforms in General - Positive Qualities

1. **Low financial barrier.** You can experiment without subscription pressure.

2. **Good for beginners.** Helpful if you are just returning to dating and want to test the waters.

3. **High variety.** You might meet individuals you would never encounter in your daily offline life.

4. **Opportunities for learning.** Navigating free spaces can teach you a great deal about your needs, boundaries, and patterns.

Why Free Platforms Might Be Good for You

They can be a training ground. A place to understand how you show up in conversation. A space to notice what drains you and what energizes you. If you enter with awareness and clear limits, they may help you grow.

Closing Thought

Santiago Dagon offers a reminder. "It is not the size of the crowd that decides your fate. It is the clarity of your own steps within it." Free dating platforms will likely remain noisy and unpredictable. Yet if you move through them with calm eyes, firm boundaries, and a steady sense of who you are, they can still lead you toward honest connection or at the very least toward deeper understanding of yourself.

CHAPTER 13

ASIAN DATING APPS AND INTERNATIONAL PLATFORMS

There is a noteworthy kind of romantic longing that reaches beyond borders. Someone sits at a kitchen table on one side of the world, scrolling through faces from another continent, and feels an attraction. The idea is simple. Perhaps love lives somewhere far away. Perhaps a person raised in a different culture might be kinder, more loyal, more traditional, or more open than the people nearby.

According to reports on global online dating trends, international and Asia-focused dating platforms have grown steadily over the past decade, as more people look beyond their own countries for romance, marriage, or companionship. These spaces can create beautiful connections. They can also expose deep power imbalances and painful patterns of exploitation.

Santiago Dagon once wrote, "When distance is great, imagination walks ahead of truth." International dating is often full of imagination. This chapter helps you see more of the truth.

CULTURAL EXPECTATIONS AND GENDER DYNAMICS

Why International Dating Attracts Certain User Types?

International dating, particularly between Western men and women from countries in Asia, Eastern Europe, Latin America, and other regions, often grows from a mixture of curiosity, romantic ideals, and cultural narratives. Many people are sincere. A Western man may believe that women from certain countries value family more deeply or hold more traditional roles. A woman from an Asian country may believe that Western men are more emotionally open, or more financially stable.

According to cross-cultural relationship research, people are often drawn to partners from other cultures when they feel disappointed with dating norms in their own environment. Some men feel that local women are too independent or disinterested in marriage. Some women feel that local men are not serious or do not commit. International platforms promise a different pool, with different expectations.

However, gender dynamics can become complicated. In some international pairings, especially those that involve large economic differences, the man may unconsciously expect obedience, gratitude, or traditional submission. The woman may feel pressure to fit these expectations in order to secure safety, financial stability, or a route to migration. None of this is always spoken aloud. It appears in small moments. Who gets to decide where they live? Who controls money? Who gives up more? And whose family is more important?

A woman from Southeast Asia once said, "She wanted a loyal kind husband, but he wanted me to be his servant." Her words reveal the hidden cultural expectations when relationship issues are not discussed openly.

THE VISA, FANTASY, AND FETISHIZATION PROBLEM

Power Imbalances and Exploitation.

When people meet across borders, visas and immigration rules enter the picture. According to international marriage and migration studies, some couples navigate this with care and equality. Others enter relationships where the visa becomes an invisible bargaining chip. The partner who controls access to a wealthier country may hold more power, even if they do not intend to move.

Visa and immigration rules can sometimes enable a double life. In these situations, a man may visit, present the appearance of commitment, then leave using visa expiration as a reason, while continuing the relationship with the option to return the following year. In some cases, the woman may also benefit through financial support and the freedom to pursue other relationships during his absence. In a conversation with a woman from another country, she disclosed that she was involved with three men, carefully managing her time so she could see each one, while each provided her with monthly financial support.

Some Western men may carry idealized images of "Asian women" as submissive, eternally grateful partners who will heal their loneliness and never challenge them. This is not respect. It is fetishization. It turns real people into objects. In dating culture, fetishization of Asian women occurs when they are reduced to stereotypes or physical traits rather than recognized as whole individuals. It treats culture, appearance, or perceived submissiveness as defining qualities, stripping away individuality.

On the other side, some women may romanticize Western men as rescuers, ticket-givers, or embodiments of a better life. They might imagine safety, comfort, and romantic gestures that differ from their experiences at home. When both sides are relating more to fantasy than to a person, disappointment is almost certain.

Santiago Dagon wrote, "When you love an idea more than a person, you build a house on mist." Fantasies about nationality, race, or culture can be very strong. But they do not survive contact with daily life. Real partnership is always specific. Two humans. Two histories. Two sets of wounds and strengths.

SCAMMERS WITHIN INTERNATIONAL PLATFORMS

Romance Fraud and Identity Theft.

Scammers are drawn to international dating spaces because distance can hide many things. According to multiple global fraud and consumer protection reports, romance scams involving cross-border relationships have become a major concern. Some scammers pretend to be from one country while living in another. Some use stolen photos of attractive people in uniforms or professional roles. Others pose as foreigners working overseas in oil rigs, construction projects, or military contracts.

International platforms can make it easier for scammers to ask for money under believable conditions. Travel emergencies, visa costs, medical bills, customs problems, and "business opportunities" are common storylines. When the victim lives far away, it is harder to verify details. It is also harder to visit in person.

In some cases, organized fraud groups reportedly train individuals to target users in specific countries, using scripts that appeal to cultural expectations, gender roles, and economic differences. Distance becomes both the hook and the shield.

A middle-aged man shared, "She said she needed help with paperwork to come to me. I sent it. Then more. By the time I realized what was happening, I was ashamed to tell anyone."

His pain was not only about the money. It was about the feeling of having his hope used against him.

THE WESTERN MAN IN SEARCH OF OBEDIENT LOYAL ASIAN LOVE

Many Western men who join Asian dating platforms are kind, respectful, and openhearted. They may simply feel drawn to cultural values that emphasize family, hospitality, and long-term commitment. They might have had painful experiences in local dating and believe that an international partner will appreciate them more fully.

However, there is another pattern. Some men arrive with a very specific fantasy. They speak about wanting a woman who "knows her place," who will never argue, who will always be loyal, who will cook, clean, and care for them with endless gratitude. They sometimes speak about "traditional Asian wives" as though they are a product category.

A Western man said, "I just want someone who will not talk back all the time. Western women are too strong." He did not sound cruel. He sounded tired. Yet the belief beneath his words was clear. He wanted relief from equality.

For a Western woman with a male partner raised in a culturally different environment, this dynamic can be dangerous. It places them in a role where their value is judged by obedience rather than mutual respect. It may limit their voice in decisions about money, travel, friendships, and work. It may also expose them to emotional or physical abuse if they ever push back.

Santiago Dagon offers a more compassionate standard, "Loyalty is not silence. It is the courage to stay honest when speaking feels risky." Real love does not require a woman to disappear. It does not require her to be obedient so that a man can feel strong.

International relationships can be beautiful. Many cross-cultural marriages thrive on trust, humor, and shared growth. But when a man seeks a partner mainly because he believes she will obey, he is not looking for a relationship. He is looking for control.

THE POSITIVE SIDE OF ASIAN DATING APPS AND INTERNATIONAL PLATFORMS

Why They Might Be Good for You?

Despite the risks, international and Asian dating platforms hold real potential for good. They are not inherently toxic. They are tools that magnify whatever intentions people bring into them. Used with clarity and respect, they can open doors to meaningful, life-changing relationships.

POSITIVE QUALITIES

1. Cross-cultural learning.

Meeting someone from another country can expand your view of family, work, faith, and daily life. You see the world through another language, another history, another rhythm.

2.   Shared values that cross borders.

Many people seek partners who value commitment, respect for elders, or spiritual life. These values exist in all cultures. International platforms can help like-hearted people find each other, even when they are far apart.

3.   Opportunities for deep intentionality.

Long-distance connections often require more communication. Time zones force you to plan. Conversations become more thoughtful because you cannot always rely on quick meetups.

4.   Healing from past experiences.

Some people find that a partner from another culture understands their pain in a different way. There is less pressure to repeat old patterns because the relationship is not rooted in shared local habits.

5.   Hope for those in limited local dating markets.

People in small towns, conservative communities, or isolated situations may discover that international platforms offer real chances for love that does not exist nearby.

WHY THESE INTERNATIONAL DATING PLATFORMS MIGHT BE GOOD FOR YOU

They might serve you well if you:

- Are genuinely curious about other cultures, and open to change in your own habits and expectations.

- Are willing to discuss power, money, family roles, and visas openly and fairly.

- Can afford to travel and are prepared to verify identity, not just trust stories.

- Want a relationship built on shared values rather than shared nationality.

- Are ready to challenge your own fantasies and stereotypes about what an "Asian partner" or "Western partner" is supposed to be.

Closing Thought

If you are a Western man considering an Asian dating platforms, it may help to ask yourself a few questions. Do I want a partner or a role? Am I prepared to listen as much as I speak? Am I willing to share power, not only provide support?

If you are an Asian woman or man meeting foreigners online, you might ask: Does this person see me as a whole human being, or as an escape from their own culture? Do they ask about my dreams, or only about my duties?

Santiago Dagon reminds us, "The border that matters most in love is not between countries, but between using and honoring." International dating can lead to many healthy, lasting relationships when both people choose respect over exploitation. That choice begins long before a plane ticket is purchased. It begins with honesty about one's intentions.

PART V

TRUTH, SAFETY, AND REAL
CONNECTION

CHAPTER 14

IS ONLINE DATING REALLY FOR YOU?

Before someone downloads a dating app, a question whispers: "Am I ready for this?" Many people skip past that question because the world moves quickly and loneliness moves even faster. Yet understanding yourself before stepping into online dating might save you from heartache, confusion, and months of emotional exhaustion.

According to psychological research on self-awareness and relational health, knowing your temperament, your emotional readiness, and your true intentions is one of the strongest predictors of successful relationship outcomes. Santiago Dagon wrote, "Most journeys fail not because the path is wrong, but because the traveler never asked where they wished to go." This chapter helps you ask where you wish to go.

TEMPERAMENT ASSESSMENT

Do You Thrive with Options or Drown in Them?

Online dating gives you choices. Many choices. Sometimes too many. Some temperaments feel energized by variety. They enjoy browsing profiles. They treat the experience with curiosity and lightness. Others feel overwhelmed. They second-guess everything. They worry they are missing someone better. They feel drained, not excited.

Ask yourself:

- Do I enjoy exploring many possibilities, or do I prefer a smaller, more focused environment?

- Do I make decisions quickly, or does too much choice create anxiety?

- Do I handle rejection with calm acceptance, or does it trigger old wounds?

- When I swipe, do I feel hopeful or tired?

A woman once said, "I thought I wanted options, but the options were choosing me. I felt lost." Her words reveal something important. Options are not always empowering. They can sometimes blur your sense of direction.

If your temperament thrives in structure and slower pacing, traditional or niche dating platforms may suit you better. If you enjoy variety and do not take things personally, broader apps might feel energizing.

EMOTIONAL AVAILABILITY TEST

Are You Ready for A Real Relationship?

Being single does not always mean being emotionally available. According to several studies on attachment and relational readiness, availability depends on your ability to trust, to communicate, and to risk being seen honestly.

Consider these questions gently:

- Am I still grieving in a past relationship?

- Do I fantasize about love more than I practice it?

- Am I open to adjusting my life for someone else?

- Can I set boundaries without fearing abandonment?

- Do I have space in my heart and schedule for a partner?

One man said, "I realized I was looking for someone to fix my loneliness, not someone to share life with." His honesty reflects a truth many feel but rarely say aloud.

Emotional availability is less about being perfect and more about being willing to remain present rather than guarded by fear.

INTENTIONS INVENTORY

Finding Your Why? Before Downloading an App.

Most people skip this part. They download because friends told them to. Or because they felt lonely on a Friday night. Or because someone else hurt them and they want to feel chosen again.

Sitting peacefully with your intentions may protect you more than any red flag list.

Ask yourself:

- Why do I want to date right now?

- Am I seeking validation, or connection?

- Am I looking for healing or distraction?

- Do I want a partner, or am I craving attention?

- Am I ready to give as much as I hope to receive?

Your Why? does not need to be perfect. It only needs to be honest. Santiago Dagon wrote, "Clarity is kindness to the self. Confusion is a slow betrayal." Knowing your intention is an act of kindness.

IF YOU ARE BURNED OUT

How To Reset and Regain Clarity.

Burnout is common. According to many surveys on online dating experiences, users often repeat the cycle of hope, disappointment, confusion, and withdrawal. If you feel drained, numb, or cynical, you may be burned out.

Signs Include:

- Feeling irritated when you open the app.

- Swiping without interest.

- Ghosting because you have no energy.

- Believing everyone has bad intentions.

- Feeling unattractive or unworthy.

- Staying on apps out of habit, not hope.

To Reset:

- Take a full break for thirty days.

- Delete the apps, not just hide them.

- Spend time with friends, books, nature, creativity.

- Reflect on what hurts you and what taught you.

- Create a new intention before returning.

A woman said, "I deleted everything. I needed silence to hear myself again." Silence can be a healing friend.

Closing Thought

Santiago Dagon closes this chapter with a simple truth. "Before you ask who you might meet, ask who you are becoming." Online dating is not just about finding someone. It is about finding clarity within yourself. When that clarity arrives, connection follows more naturally, whether through an app or through the unfolding of life itself.

CHAPTER 15

HOW TO PROTECT YOURSELF ONLINE

There is a straightforward truth that many people discover only after they have been hurt. Safety is not something the app can give you. Safety is awareness you must carry with you. Every time you open your phone. Every time you answer a message. Every time you feel your heart lean forward toward a stranger you have not met yet.

According to multiple consumer protection and cybercrime agencies, online dating can be used both for genuine connection and for exploitation. Dating platforms are tools. They are not policing agencies or security protection companies. What happens inside them depends on the intentions of the people who show up there. Santiago Dagon once wrote, "The world will not always be gentle with your heart, so you must learn how to stand gently guard over it."

This chapter is about guarding your heart. Not building a wall. Not paranoia. A thoughtful protection that allows you to stay open to love without abandoning yourself.

PSYCHOLOGICAL SELF-DEFENSE

Discernment, Boundary-Setting, Emotional Stability

Psychological self-defense starts inside your own mind. It is not about becoming hard or cynical. It is about developing discernment. The ability to notice how someone's words affect you. The ability to listen to that small warning whisper inside your chest when something feels off.

Ask Yourself as You Interact:

- How do I feel after I talk to this person? Calmer or more anxious.

- Do I feel respected? Or do I feel pushed, rushed, or cornered.

- Am I allowed to say No without being punished?

- Does this person listen, or do they only talk about themselves?

Healthy boundary-setting means you know where your lines are. For example:

- I will not share personal details before I feel comfortable.

- I will not continue chatting with someone who insults me or pressures me.

- I will not move off the app or meet in person until certain basic checks are done.

- I will step away if my body feels tense and my mind feels confused.

One woman said, "I used to think boundaries would scare people away. Now I understand they protect me from the wrong people and attract the right ones." Her shift is important. Setting boundaries does not mean being unkind. They are a form of self-respect.

Emotional stability does not mean you never feel hurt or lonely. It means you do not let those feelings drive desperate decisions. When you are tired or fragile, you may pause before responding. You may sleep on a big decision. You may check your feelings with a trusted friend. Santiago Dagon wrote, "The heart that pauses before it gives itself is not cold. It is wise."

PRACTICAL DIGITAL SAFETY

Identity Protection, Data Minimization, Profile Hygiene

Practical safety is the unglamorous side of online dating. According to cyber security guidance from many official organizations, protecting your identity and minimizing shared data significantly reduces your risk.

Some simple practices:

Limit Personal Information on Your Profile.

Avoid listing your full name, exact home address, work address, or very specific daily routines. There is no need to share your children's names or schools. General is safer than exact.

Use Different Photos Than Your Main Social Media Profiles.

If someone can easily reverse search your dating photos and find your full name, workplace, and family in one click, you lose an important layer of privacy.

Be Careful with Contact Details.

Consider using app messaging until you feel safe. When you move to another platform, such as a messaging app, think about what that platform reveals about you. Email addresses that contain your full name or workplace can give away more than you intend.

Avoid Sending Sensitive Images.

Intimate photos or videos can be saved, copied, or used in coercive ways. If someone pressures you to send such content early, this is a red flag, not a sign of intimacy.

Profile Hygiene.

Review your profile and privacy settings regularly. Remove information that no longer feels wise to share. Update photos so that they reflect you, but do not expose unnecessary details about your environment.

A man once said, "I used to treat my profile like a résumé. Now I treat it like a first hello." That shift in mindset can help. You do not need to reveal everything at the door.

FINANCIAL SAFETY

How To Avoid Being Exploited or Manipulated.

Financial safety is one of the clearest lines you can draw. According to statistics reported by consumer protection agencies, romance scams involving money requests cost victims large sums every year. The patterns are often similar. A crisis appears. A plea for help follows. Emotional pressure rises.

Some core rules that may protect you:

- Do not send money to someone you have never met in person, no matter how convincing the story might feel.

- Do not share banking information, credit card numbers, or copies of identity documents.

- Be cautious with investment opportunities introduced by new romantic interests, especially in areas such as cryptocurrency, foreign exchange, or "guaranteed" high returns.

- Do not buy gift cards, transfer funds, or pay third parties on someone's behalf because of a story that began in an app.

Common scam storylines include:

- A sudden medical emergency.

- A business deal stuck in customs.

- A family member who needs urgent help.

- Travel problems that require immediate funds.

- A request for help to unlock an inheritance.

One woman said, "He told me I was the only one he trusted. I believed him. I wanted to be that person for him." Her desire to be important made her vulnerable. Scammers often use flattery and emotional intimacy to lower a victim's defenses.

You are smart if you refuse financial requests. You are safeguarding both your resources and your dignity.

TRUST SLOWLY, VERIFY EVERYTHING

Healthy Skepticism vs. Paranoia.

There is a difference between healthy skepticism and fear. Healthy skepticism says, "I will take my time and check what I can." Paranoia says, "No one can be trusted at all." You do not need to live in paranoia to be safe. You can live in careful trust.

Practical verification steps:

- Suggest a quick video call before meeting in person. A genuine person might feel shy, but they will usually agree.

- Notice whether their stories stay consistent over time.

- Look for an online presence that roughly matches what they tell you.

- Meet for the first time in public spaces.

- Tell a friend where you are going and share a screenshot of the profile.

If someone resists any form of verification, you may take that as information. Not proof, but information. A man once said, "The moment she refused a video call three times, I stopped making excuses for her." That decision might have saved him from deeper harm.

Santiago Dagon wrote, "Trust can be a bridge, but every bridge must rest on something solid." Verification is simply the care taken to ensure that what you are building will endure.

SCAMMERS ARE MEN, WOMEN, AND TRANSGENDER; IN EVERY AGE GROUP; IN ALL NATIONALITIES; IN ALL DATING APPS

It is important to be very clear here. Scammers do not belong to one gender, one country, one culture, or one age group. According to global fraud and cybercrime reports, people of all identities have been involved in online romance scams and emotional exploitation. Men scam. Women scam. Transgender people scam. Every country and age group have scammers.

The danger in stereotyping is simple. When you assume that only a certain type of person scams, you lower your guard with others. That false sense of security can create more risk, not less.

Scammers can appear:

- Kind.

- Sophisticated.

- Spiritual.

- Educated.

- Poor.

- Wealthy.

- Local.

- Foreign.

They may say the right things. They may quote sacred texts or therapy language. They may talk about healing, trauma, or growth. They might appear in niche faith-based apps, serious relationship platforms, casual hookup spaces, and free social networks. There is no category that is immune.

One man said, "I thought only men scammed women. Then I lost money to someone who played on my loneliness after my divorce." Another person shared, "I trusted her because she talked so much about God. I did not notice the inconsistency in her stories." Repeatedly, people describe how love clouded their judgment and how that trust was later broken through financial exploitation.

Santiago Dagon offers a different way to see it. "Do not judge the risk by the face in front of you. Judge it by the weight it places on your spirit." If a connection feels heavy, pressured, rushed, or confusing, that is your signal, regardless of who the person is or where they come from.

Closing Thought

Take a moment to notice how you feel right now. Perhaps more cautious. Perhaps calmer. Real safety does not create fear or panic. It creates clarity about what you will accept and what you will refuse.

You are allowed to protect your heart. You are allowed to go slowly. You are allowed to say no. And you are allowed to hope for a connection grounded in the same care you are learning to extend to yourself.

CHAPTER 16

ALTERNATIVES TO ONLINE DATING FOR FINDING TRUE LOVE

There is a sense of relief when someone realizes that online dating is not the only way to love. Many people feel trapped between loneliness and a screen, as if all modern connection must come through an app. But love existed before profiles. Before swipes. Before algorithms. It grew in everyday places where people lived real lives and saw each other fully.

According to relationship research and community studies, meaningful partnerships often begin in spaces where people share values, activities, or mutual purpose. Santiago Dagon wrote, "Love often enters through the side door, not the front gate." This chapter opens those side doors.

REAL-WORLD CONNECTION STRATEGIES

Events, Hobbies, Social Circles, Shared-Interest Communities.

Real-world connections grow differently than online introductions. It often begins with shared context. A class. A conversation. A moment of laughter. You see not just what the person looks like but how they behave, how they listen, how they treat others around them.

Some places where authentic connection might grow:

- Book clubs, writing groups, or creative circles.

- Hiking groups, yoga classes, dance lessons.

- Cooking classes, gardening clubs, language meetups.

- Local lectures, community festivals, art openings.

- Fitness communities or group sports.

- Neighborhood gatherings or alumni events.

A man once said, "When I met her in a photography class, I saw who she was before I knew her name." His eyes relaxed as he spoke. That is the magic of real-world environments. They reveal character before chemistry, which may create a deeper foundation.

Joining these spaces does not guarantee romance. They are not designed for dating. And perhaps that is why they work. People act more naturally when they are not performing for a romantic outcome.

MATCHMAKING AND PERSONAL INTRODUCTIONS

Coaching-Guided Introductions, Curated Dating.

Matchmaking might sound old-fashioned, yet according to several modern relationship services, curated introductions have returned with renewed popularity. People are tired of sifting through hundreds of profiles. They want quality over quantity. They want intention.

Professional matchmakers or relationship coaches may:

- Vet both individuals before introducing them.

- Explore compatibility factors such as lifestyle, communication style, and long-term goals.

- Help clients clarify what they truly want.

- Support them as they navigate early interactions.

- Remove the overwhelm of constant searching.

These services can be costly, but some people find comfort in knowing that someone is guiding the process with care. There is also the simpler version. Personal introductions from trusted friends or colleagues. A tender, "I know someone you might like."

A woman told me, "I met my partner through a friend. She said, "You two think the same way about life. She was right." Her smile revealed the power of someone who sees you clearly enough to introduce you with intention.

FAITH-BASED OR VALUES-BASED COMMUNITIES

Where Aligned Belief Sets Reduce Risk and Increase Bonding.

Shared values create a closer bond kind of intimacy. Faith-based communities, cultural groups, or organizations built around service often bring together people who hold similar beliefs about family, commitment, spirituality, ethics, or life purpose.

Examples include:

- Church, temple, or mosque communities.

- Meditation centers or spiritual learning groups.

- Volunteer ministries.

- Cultural associations.

- Faith-based singles gatherings.

- Value-oriented clubs and circles.

According to many relationship studies, couples who share core values often experience more alignment in decision-making and long-term satisfaction. It does not mean the relationship is perfect. It means the soil beneath it is rich.

A man said, "We met at a small spiritual workshop. We both believed in kindness more than perfection. That was enough to begin." His tone carried a peace that many people seek.

These communities are not dating pools. They are shared homes of meaning. Love often grows there because people meet each other in the presence of something they both care about deeply.

FRIENDSHIP-FIRST MODELS

Slow Connection, Organic Growth, Compatibility Over Chemistry.

There is a particular strength in relationships that begin as friendships. According to social and relational research, many long-term couples start in friendship because they build emotional safety before romantic intensity. There is less performance. Less pressure. More authenticity.

A friendship-first approach may include:

- Getting to know someone slowly.

- Allowing attraction to grow gradually.

- Watching how they treat people when romance is not the goal.

- Building trust before commitment.

- Not rushing into defining the relationship.

One woman said, "It felt easy. There was no sparkle at first, just comfort. The sparkle came later." Her story reminds us that chemistry can grow when two people genuinely like each other.

Friendship-first connection reduces risk because you see the person more clearly. You see their consistency. Their character. Their habits. You are not blinded by instant passion, which sometimes creates unrealistic expectations.

Santiago Dagon wrote, "A slow flame often burns the longest." There is wisdom in that.

VOLUNTEERING, WORKSHOPS, AND LEARNING GROUPS

High-Quality Environments to Meet Grounded People.

Volunteering or learning spaces often attract individuals who care about growth, service, or contribution. These qualities tend to create healthier relational foundations. According to community engagement studies, volunteering can increase life satisfaction, emotional resilience, and social bonding.

Some meaningful settings include:

- Habitat for Humanity builds.

- Animal shelters.

- Food banks or community kitchens.

- Environmental clean-up groups.

- Educational workshops.

- Wellness retreats.

- Professional development seminars.

- Mindfulness or personal-growth workshops.

Meeting someone in a place of service can reveal their compassion. Meeting someone in a learning environment can reveal their humility and curiosity. These traits often matter more than physical attraction or shared hobbies.

A man shared, "I met her at a weekend workshop about communication. We both wanted to grow. That told me more than any dating profile could." His insight was clear.

People who invest in themselves often invest in their relationships as well.

Closing Thought

As you consider these alternatives, notice what feels possible. Notice what sparks. Notice what relaxes your heart. Online dating is one pathway, not the only one.

Santiago Dagon leaves us with this reflection: "Love does not hide. It waits in the places where your life is already speaking."

Sometimes the place that speaks to you is an app. Sometimes it is a community garden. A small workshop. A peaceful café where you read the same book for weeks. True love often appears when your life becomes spacious enough for it to enter.

Walk into the spaces that nourish you. Love may already be standing there.

CHAPTER 17

WHAT REAL LOVE REQUIRES THAT DATING APPS CANNOT GIVE

In every modern love story, there comes a point when someone realizes that an app can only take them so far. A swipe might introduce two people, but it cannot hold their hearts together. A match can spark excitement, but it cannot create the soil where trust grows. Technology might open the door, but real love asks you to step inside with your whole being.

According to countless interviews with couples, therapists, and relationship researchers, lasting love depends on qualities that no app can manufacture. Santiago Dagon wrote, "A doorway can invite you in. The home is built by your hands." This chapter explores what those hands must build.

SLOWNESS

Why Love Grows Through Time, Not Swipes.

Real love does not rush. It unfolds. It stretches. It breathes.

Dating apps encourage quick impressions. Quick decisions. Quick exits. Yet the human heart does not work in quick mode.

It takes time to feel safe. Time to see patterns. Time to understand someone's joys, wounds, and rhythms.

Ask yourself:

- Do I allow things to grow naturally, or do I demand instant clarity?

- Do I feel anxious when progress is slow?

- Do I confuse excitement with compatibility?

A woman once told me, "He was slow and steady. I kept waiting for fireworks. Then one day I realized I trusted him more than anyone." Her realization captured the nature of real love. Slow can be steady. Steady can be beautiful.

Apps can introduce you. Only time can reveal who someone truly is.

DEPTH

Apps Reward Superficiality; Relationships Demand Depth.

According to numerous studies on digital dating psychology, apps often push people to focus on appearance, wit, and surface traits. Yet genuine relationships require much more. Depth arises when two people:

- Share fears and dreams.

- Apologize sincerely.

- Navigate conflict without destroying each other.

- Listen without planning a response.

- Reveal the parts of themselves that they wish were easier to love.

Depth requires vulnerability. Stillness. Patience. It happens in conversations that take longer than a few minutes. Love grows when you begin to understand the layers beneath the profile.

Santiago Dagon wrote, "Two shallow rivers cannot form an ocean. Depth comes when both choose to go below the surface." Apps can show the surface. Depth is something you must create together.

VULNERABILITY

Impossible To Fake Via Chat Bubbles.

Vulnerability is one of the clearest markers of real emotional presence. It might include:

- Sharing an insecurity.

- Admitting a past mistake.

- Asking for reassurance.

- Telling someone what you need.

- Revealing the truth of a wound.

Text messages cannot hold the weight of real vulnerability. They can hint at it. They can gesture toward it. But vulnerability lives in tone, in silence, in eye contact, and in the courage of being seen.

One man said, "I realized I could tell her when I felt anxious. That was when I knew it was real." His statement reveals something powerful. Love expands where vulnerability is welcomed.

Apps cannot teach vulnerability. They cannot guarantee it. They can only connect two people willing to practice it.

SHARED LIFE CONTEXT

Why Real-World Environments Build Stronger Bonds.

Shared context creates belonging. According to relationship researchers, people bond more deeply when they spend time in shared environments. Not virtual ones. Real ones. Life unfolds through:

- Errands.

- Meals.

- Work schedules.

- Family traditions.

- Habits and routines.

- Weather and seasons.

- Daily decisions.

When two people move through real-world experiences together, they discover compatibility that apps cannot measure. They learn how the other person behaves when tired, stressed, disappointed, or joyful. They learn how generosity shows up in action, not words.

A woman said, "I fell in love with how he carried groceries for his elderly neighbor. That told me who he was more than any profile ever could." Daily life reveals character in small ways.

Apps can start a story. Real life writes it.

COMMITMENT AND FOLLOW-THROUGH

The Ultimate Filter: Consistency

According to research on healthy relationships, consistency is one of the strongest predictors of long-term success. A person may say anything. The real question is whether they follow through. Commitment shows itself through:

- Showing up when they said they would.

- Being dependable in communication.

- Balancing independence with connection.

- Choosing you even when things feel imperfect.

- Repairing after conflict.

Commitment is measured in actions, not promises. One man said, "She kept choosing me, even on the days when I was not easy." That is what real love looks like. Not ease. Intentionality. Apps can create moments. Commitment creates movement.

SIGNS THAT A PERSON IS SERIOUS ABOUT HAVING TRUE LOVE IN THEIR LIFE

Seriousness Reveals Itself Quietly.

Look For Signs That Someone Is Ready for Something Real:

- They communicate openly and respectfully.

- They ask thoughtful questions.

- They show curiosity about your values, not just your appearance.

- They initiate plans and follow through.

- They maintain steady effort.

- They set healthy boundaries and respect yours.

- They do not disappear when things become inconvenient.

- They speak about the future in a grounded, realistic way.

- They show emotional availability, not emotional chaos.

- They demonstrate stability in friendships, work, and lifestyle.

- Their words and actions align over time.

A serious person does not rush, but they do not leave you confused. They create clarity by being consistent.

Santiago Dagon wrote, "Love is a promise that reveals itself in small daily choices." Watch those choices carefully.

CHECKLIST OF TRUE LOVE QUALITIES TO MEASURE YOUR POTENTIAL PARTNER

Use This Checklist Gently, Not Rigidly. It Is Not a Test.
It Is a Guide to Help You See Someone More Clearly.

Emotional Qualities

- Does this person handle stress without cruelty?

- Do they apologize when wrong?

- Do they listen when you speak?

- Do they show empathy?

- Do they respect emotional boundaries?

Behavioral Qualities

- Are they consistent?

- Do they follow through on commitments?

- Do their daily habits align with a stable life?

- Are they trustworthy with time, money, and secrets?

Relational Qualities

- Do they value connection over ego?

- Do they maintain healthy relationships with friends and family?

- Do they make space for you without abandoning themselves?

- Do they communicate honestly even when it is uncomfortable?

Compatibility Indicators

- Do your values align?

- Do your lifestyles complement each other?

- Do your long-term goals fit together?

- Do you feel safe, not anxious, around them?

If you find yourself checking most of the boxes, you might be building something meaningful. If many remain unchecked, perhaps the relationship needs deeper evaluation.

QUESTIONS TO ASK YOUR POTENTIAL PARTNER BEFORE GETTING SERIOUS

These Questions Invite Emotional Honesty and Help Reveal Compatibility:

Values and Lifestyle

- What does a healthy relationship mean to you?

- How do you handle conflict?

- What role does family play in your life?

- How do you manage money?

- What are your long-term goals?

Emotional Presence

- What have past relationships taught you?

- How do you take care of your mental and emotional health?

- What do you need from a partner when you feel overwhelmed?

Commitment and Intention

- What makes you feel ready for a long-term relationship?

- How do you balance independence with partnership?

- What type of future are you hoping to build with someone?

Compatibility and Daily Life

- What does a peaceful day look like to you?

- How do you prioritize time with people you love?

- How do you want to grow in the next five years?

Ask slowly. Ask gently. Ask with genuine curiosity. The right person will not fear these questions. They will welcome them.

Closing Thought

Santiago Dagon closes the chapter with a plain truth. "Love is not found by speed or strategy. It is found when two honest lives move toward each other with patience."

Apps can help you meet. They cannot help you love. Love requires depth, vulnerability, slowness, context, and commitment. These are not digital skills. They are human ones. They rise only when two people are willing to bring their whole selves to the relationship.

CHAPTER 18

DATING TIPS FOR EACH GENERATION GROUP

SILENT GENERATION ONLINE DATING TIPS

(Those born 1925 - 1945)

Members of this generation may prioritize companionship, emotional steadiness, and genuine conversation. Technology may feel overwhelming, but curiosity remains.

Tips:

- Choose platforms designed for seniors with simpler interfaces.

- Verify identity through video before meeting.

- Meet in public spaces with family informed.

- Trust slow pacing.

- Share your boundaries clearly.

- Do not hesitate to involve adult children for safety support.

Online dating might feel foreign. But companionship is timeless.

BOOMER GENERATION ONLINE DATING TIPS

(Born 1946 - 1964)

Boomers often enter dating after divorce or widowhood. According to research on later-life dating, many seek companionship rather than intense romance.

Tips:

- Use senior-focused platforms, which attract more serious users.

- Watch for scammers targeting older adults.

- Set emotional pace intentionally.

- Stay honest about health, lifestyle, and expectations.

- Embrace new beginnings without rushing.

Boomers often bring wisdom and maturity into dating. Use that strength.

GENERATION X ONLINE DATING TIPS

(Born 1965 - 1980)

Gen X often balances work, children, and emotional healing. This generation may feel skeptical but still hopeful.

Tips:

- Choose platforms with strong filtering options.

- Be honest about parenting responsibilities.

- Do not compete with younger daters. Play your strengths.

- Set boundaries around communication pace.

- Watch for partners in midlife crisis stages.

Gen Xers often make excellent partners when they feel emotionally secure.

MILLENNIALS' ONLINE DATING TIPS

(Born 1981 - 1996)

Millennials grew up alongside the internet. Many are familiar with apps and social media but may feel tired of superficiality.

Tips:

- Choose apps that encourage depth (Hinge, Match, etc.).

- Avoid falling into constant comparison or FOMO.

- Seek partners who value emotional intelligence.

- Set boundaries around texting vs. actual dates.

- Notice patterns, not words.

Millennials often want both passion and partnership. That balance takes intention.

Z GENERATION ONLINE DATING TIPS

(Born 1997 - 2012)

Gen Z is digitally fluent but emotionally vulnerable. According to early studies, this generation experiences more anxiety and depression linked to online social dynamics.

Tips:

- Protect mental health by limiting app time.

- Prioritize emotional safety over aesthetic perfection.

- Verify identity early.

- Avoid bonding through trauma-sharing too fast.

- Do not chase external validation.

- Practice self-worth before seeking partnership.

Gen Z may redefine modern love by blending authenticity with digital awareness.

CONCLUSION

A Clearer Path to Real Love

At the end of any meaningful inquiry, there is a moment of recognition. You see more clearly than before. Not with fear, but with understanding. Something in you has sharpened.

Online dating is now one of the most common ways people meet. It is also one of the most misunderstood. Beneath the polished profiles and curated images sits a layered ecosystem shaped by algorithms, incentives, loneliness, hope, and at times deception. You now understand what operates behind the screen. The business structures. The behavioral patterns. The motivations that range from sincere to misleading.

Apps are tools. They are not saviors. They can open a door, but they cannot build trust, character, or emotional maturity. Those qualities still belong to human beings.

Perhaps the greatest insight is this: the modern search for love requires both heart and discernment. It requires emotional boundaries, digital awareness, and patience. It asks you to recognize that behind every profile is a person, but not always the full truth. It asks you to see clearly without becoming hardened.

Scammers do not belong to one gender, one age group, or one culture. Loneliness does not either. On these platforms gather the hopeful, the healing, the confused, the unavailable, the deceptive, and the deeply sincere. The challenge is not avoiding the search. It is learning to navigate it wisely.

You may notice something has shifted in you. Less urgency. More steadiness. A stronger ability to distinguish intention from illusion. Santiago Dagon once wrote, "Love reveals itself to the one who stands calmly with open hands, not to the one who grasps wildly in the dark." Clarity does not close the heart. It steadies it.

Approaching online dating with awareness does not mean fearing it. It means moving with intention. It means understanding that safety is not suspicion. It is self respect. It means allowing trust to grow slowly and verifying what matters.

We write this as two voices, male and female, united in one observation: real love still exists. It is not defeated by technology. But it is not guaranteed by it either. It requires patience, honesty, and emotional courage from both people involved.

No book can promise you partnership. But awareness changes outcomes. When you understand the environment, you change how you move within it.

Move forward with open eyes. Speak honestly. Protect yourself without closing yourself. Choose those who choose you back. And remember that real love is not found in perfect profiles, but in two imperfect people willing to meet beyond the screen.

ACKNOWLEDGEMENTS

This book exists because many individuals were willing to speak honestly about experiences that are often private, complicated, and emotionally charged.

We are grateful to the women and men we encountered throughout our own journeys in the world of online dating. Each conversation, whether brief or ongoing, revealed something deeply human beneath the profiles and algorithms. Those encounters shaped our understanding in ways no dataset alone could.

We also thank the individuals who shared their stories candidly, sometimes at personal cost. Many spoke not to assign blame, but to better understand disappointment, hope, misunderstanding, vulnerability, and resilience. Others offered insight quietly, without expectation of recognition, trusting that their experiences might help someone else navigate more wisely.

This work also stands on the careful foundation laid by researchers, graduate students, and academic institutions who have examined online dating, digital intimacy, loneliness, trust, and deception. Their scholarship illuminated patterns that personal stories alone cannot fully explain.

To all who contributed perspective, caution, and courage, we extend our sincere gratitude.

ABOUT AUTHORS

Amelia L. Starwell is a cultural and spiritual author whose work explores longing, belief, and the inner forces that shape human relationships. Drawing from spiritual traditions, lived experience, and careful cultural observation, she writes with clarity and restraint. Her voice creates space for reflection rather than reaction. In examining modern connection, she brings a grounded female perspective shaped by insight, discernment, and compassion.

Nicholas J. Matyas is an American writer, educator, and cultural observer whose work examines how people search for meaning in a rapidly changing world. His writing moves between lived experience and investigative inquiry, exploring the intersection of technology, belief, and human behavior. With more than four decades of direct observation across generations and cultures, his work combines research, personal encounter, and long-form analysis.

Santiago Dagon is the contemplative voice and pen name through which Nicholas J. Matyas gives shape to deeper philosophical reflection. Writing as Dagon allows him to step beyond a single viewpoint and speak from the space where history, spirit, and human experience meet. Over time, the name has come to represent a guiding principle: that wisdom grows through reflection, that clarity requires patience, and that compassion and discernment are not opposites.

Together, Amelia L. Starwell and Nicholas J. Matyas write with complementary perspectives, blending cultural investigation with reflective insight. Their work seeks not to inflame fear, but to illuminate understanding. Within *WHO'S REALLY ON THESE DATING APPS*, they examine modern digital courtship with clear eyes, balanced judgment, and a shared commitment to honesty.

Their books are part of **The Discovery Walkabout Collection Of Reflective Writing**, a series dedicated to thoughtful inquiry into modern life, relationships, and human meaning.

To learn more about their work, visit Discovery Walkabout Press at https://discoverywalkabout.com

DISCOVERY WALKABOUT PRESS

Discovery Walkabout Press was founded on a simple belief: reflection is not a retreat from life, but a deeper way of living it.

Our mission is to create thoughtful media that nurture awareness, emotional intelligence, and understanding across generations. We publish books, articles, reflective guides, modern parables, contemplative workbooks, and seminars that invite readers to rediscover peace, purpose, curiosity, and meaningful connection. We seek work that helps people live more consciously, love more honestly, and recognize the extraordinary within everyday life.

Each title published under Discovery Walkabout Press carries a shared philosophy: learning begins in stillness, wisdom grows through relationship, and creativity expands when the mind is clear. We support projects that bridge the spiritual and the practical, encouraging readers to walk thoughtfully through their questions rather than rush toward quick conclusions.

At its heart, Discovery Walkabout Press is committed to mindful storytelling. We value depth over noise, clarity over reaction, and conversation over certainty. Our work explores modern culture, relationships, inner development, and the human search for meaning.

As a publishing house and creative development studio, we welcome collaboration with new and established authors, storytellers, researchers, and educators who share this spirit. If you are developing a manuscript, reflective project, or cultural inquiry that aligns with our values, we invite you to connect with us. Growth happens in dialogue, and we believe meaningful work is strengthened through partnership.

To learn more about our current titles and collaborative opportunities, visit: https://discoverywalkabout.com

"We do not find truth by running faster. We find it by learning how to walk with wonder."

- Santiago Dagon